Empire of Norma

'This groundbreaking book fills a crucial gap in the discourse about neuro-diversity, providing a deep history of the invention of the "normal" mind as one of the most damaging and oppressive tools of capitalism, while not suc-cumbing to the myths of the "anti-psychiatry" movement. To read it is to see the world more clearly.'
—Steve Silberman, author of *NeuroTribes: The Legacy of Autism and the Future of Neurodiversity*

'*Empire of Normality* argues that a radical politics of neurodiversity needs to be central to the struggle against capitalism. Chapman explains why this is necessary, not only for neurodivergent folk, but for our collective liberation. Thought provoking, challenging and compelling.'
—Professor Hel Spandler, Editor, *Asylum: The Radical Mental Health Magazine*

'Engaging, impeccably researched, and a vital step in the emergence of a new social paradigm. Chapman uncovers the origins of the stifling norms that limit our collective potentials, and points the way toward a better and more creative future.'
—Nick Walker, author of *Neuroqueer Heresies*

'A vital book that kindles the flames of a Marxist neurodivergent revolution. Chapman boldly challenges us to envision a world liberated from neuronor-mative oppression, where dismantling capitalism is central to disabled, Mad, and neurodivergent liberation – a new radical approach to neurodiversity that is explicitly anti-capitalist.'
—Beatrice Adler-Bolton, co-author of *Health Communism* and co-host, Death Panel podcast

'An instant seminal text, *Empire of Normality* takes on the huge task of crafting a coherent, radical, Marxist approach to neurodivergence. Chapman impressively and critically assembles disparate philosophical, scientific and activist currents across time to carve out a new politics that pushes beyond liberal rights-based approaches, and guides us towards a liberated future.'
—Micha Frazer-Carroll, author of *Mad World*

Empire of Normality

Neurodiversity and Capitalism

Robert Chapman

First published 2023 by Pluto Press
New Wing, Somerset House, Strand, London WC2R 1LA
and Pluto Press, Inc.
1930 Village Center Circle, 3-834, Las Vegas, NV 89134

www.plutobooks.com

British Library Cataloguing in Publication Data
A catalogue record for this book is available from the British Library

ISBN 978 0 7453 4866 7 Paperback
ISBN 978 0 7453 4868 1 PDF
ISBN 978 0 7453 4867 4 EPUB
ISBN 978 0 7453 4929 9 Audio

This book is printed on paper suitable for recycling and made from fully
managed and sustained forest sources. Logging, pulping and manufacturing
processes are expected to conform to the environmental standards of the
country of origin.

Typeset by Stanford DTP Services, Northampton, England

Simultaneously printed in the United Kingdom and United States of America

Contents

For Alice

Preface

In this book I use neurodiversity theory as a lens for reinterpreting the past to better navigate the present. History, after all, is useful not just for allowing us to understand what has already been. It equally gives us tools to spot patterns, traps, and possibilities in the here and now. In some cases, this can help us imagine new worlds. Perhaps more rarely, it can help us see how to bring these worlds into being. In line with such possibilities, my project here looks backwards while striving forwards. It uses history to develop an understanding that may help us collectively work towards neurodivergent liberation.

While this is a scholarly work, it is also personal and political. My thinking, inevitably, has been moulded by my experience of being neurodivergent as well as of mental illness, not to mention the stigma and discrimination that accompany these. Equally, my views and commitments have been profoundly shaped by the experience of growing up in poverty, sometimes homeless, and then in foster care in the United Kingdom. And no less important has been living through constant crises of capitalism and the mental health effects of precarious employment and insecure housing through much of my adult life. Through this and so much more, I have come to see neurodivergent oppression as bound up with the malaises of advanced capitalism as well as with the other systems of domination that capital developed alongside and remains intertwined with.

My perspective is also limited by my positionality. I am a white person born in Britain. Here I have focused most centrally on the European and North American contexts, these being the contexts I am best qualified to comment on. To an extent this is fitting as both the systems and ideas the neurodiversity movement arose to fight against, and the movement itself, are largely products of the Global North. Yet the forms of domination the movement arose to resist have had far-reaching consequences, including across much of the Global South. As I make clear throughout, the idea of the 'normal' person, brain, and mind has been intimately intertwined with colonialism, imperialism, and white supremacy. While I seek to make such connections salient, my analysis will still likely be of more direct relevance to those living in post-Fordist, high-tech economies. The extent to which it will be relevant to other contexts will depend on countless factors. My hope is that my argument will at least serve as a basis for building or contrasting different analyses that draw on different knowledges and for different contexts.

Caveats aside, my aim here is to develop a more radical analysis of neurodiversity history, theory, and politics, built from a broadly Marxian perspective. This begins with a materialist interpretation of the history of neurodivergent disablement and our understanding of normality and disability. I seek to place them within the broader context of a range of interlocking systems of domination, most centrally capitalism. In turn, while I locate the origins of the problem much earlier, I suggest that especially since the mid-twentieth century, capitalism has reached a stage where neurological domination, through either disablement or alienation, has become pervasive regardless of how close or far each of us sits to the neurotypical ideal. In an important sense, what I want to show is that capitalism's domination shifts more towards the neuronormative the further capitalism itself intensifies. Here we see a dialectical tension between the expansion of the domain of capital alongside a simultaneous restriction of neuronormativity that accompanies it.

In covering this, I hope partly to show that things are as they are not due to natural necessity, but specific historical and economic conditions. By the same token, I show that things do not have to be as they are, and that by placing neurodiversity theory and praxis within broader anti-capitalist struggles, we might help make them otherwise. This is not an attempt to offer a fully developed political strategy, since I think that is something to be done collectively, and which we are only now beginning to be ready for. Rather, it is an attempt to help develop a historical neurodivergent consciousness in such a way that will make collective efforts to develop strategy more possible. The first aim of this book is thus to uncover a past that has been rendered opaque. And the second aim is to help open up a future that we cannot yet fully understand, yet which is important to try to reach for, nonetheless.

Introduction

My life has been structured by both neurodivergence and economic hardship since the beginning. This dates to my first memories, which take place during the early 1990s in London. One characteristic impression from the council flat in which we lived is of an alcoholic father furiously ranting and raging. Another is of a distraught mother, tearfully saying goodbye as she left for some unspecified period. While there were also happier memories, home life was hard. And since we never had any money and were not part of any broader community, there seemed no realistic hope of things improving.

My impressions from school are little better. Those from the playground are mainly of bullies pointing and laughing. It was not just that I was poor and wore uncool, second-hand clothes. It was also that I was weird, quiet, and hadn't yet developed the social fluency required to evade their efforts. I also experienced constant sensory processing problems that hindered my learning. My memories of lessons are mainly of trying to strive through sensory bombardment just to hear the teacher's voice. Despite these efforts, I still often struggled to grasp even basic things. I was soon taken by my teachers to simply be lazy and unintelligent. In time they stopped trying to help, and I began to internalise their negative images of me.

Much later, I learned clinical names for these problems, and moreover, that I was far from alone in encountering them. The addiction and depression I had seen in family members, for instance, were relatively common mental health problems. I also found out that my sensory processing and social understanding issues were associated with autism, a diagnosis that had increased nationwide by 787% between 1998 and 2018.[1] I likewise discovered that my early traumatic experiences led to what is often called complex Post Traumatic Stress. More generally, I learned, related experiences of anxiety[2] and depression[3] had risen in recent decades. And the risks

1

of such problems were much higher for members of economically deprived and marginalised groups.[4] Knowing all this would later help me begin to see that my problems were not merely individual. Rather, I was suffering from wider, more systemic problems that were affecting many of us in similar ways.

Yet while all this helped my understanding in retrospect, as a child and teenager, I knew none of this. I did know I was different from those considered 'normal'. But I felt too much shame to explore what this difference might consist in, or whether it was necessarily a bad thing. At the time, the disposition of my experience was largely one of confusion, anxiety, and hopelessness. In the end, stuck in poverty, alienated from both myself and the world around me, my mental health went from bad to worse. Beyond constant anxiety and hopelessness, I developed an eating disorder, experienced intrusive thoughts, and, finally, began thinking about suicide. Life was overwhelmingly bad and there seemed no other way to escape.

As so often happens, things only began to change for the better after hitting rock bottom. This occurred, for me, in 2005, by which time I was 15. By then, I had dropped out of school and had been sleeping on the streets for some time. I had turned my back on a world that had failed me, and was initially determined to make my own way, mainly by selling cannabis for a local dealer. Yet homelessness was hard, dangerous, and lonely. And when it finally got cold enough to snow, I knew I couldn't survive. With nowhere else to go, and finally feeling defeated, I turned up at the local government council offices one cold winter morning. There, I explained my situation and asked if they could help. After an emergency meeting with a team of social workers, they decided I needed to enter the foster care system without delay. They soon found me a family to stay with in a tiny rural village miles away from anywhere I had ever been.

It was here that things began to change. First, I was dropped off at a beautiful old country house that seemed like it came straight out of a fairy-tale. In turn, I was warmly welcomed in by a new family, a white cat, and a black dog. It was in this context that I first came to experience uncomplicated encouragement, love, and support. Although this transition was far from easy, and while my disabilities and trauma remained an ongoing problem, I soon became part of the family.

From this point on, old possibilities closed off as new paths began to open. Having no schoolwork and little else to do in the village, I began to read voraciously. I also began to think about options for the future. This included, for the first time, the thought of university, which, to my surprise, seemed to be considered normal in middle-class families. After trying various subjects over the next few years, and since I found the world so chaotic and confusing, I was drawn towards the study of philosophy. My hope was that analysing concepts and social theory would help me understand and navigate the strange and chaotic world I lived in. I wanted to make sense of life and all the problems I had encountered, so I could learn to live a better life than my parents.

In the end, however, it took seven more years to find what I was looking for. By this time, I had received a long-awaited autism diagnosis and was studying philosophy while working factory nightshifts. Thankfully, much of what I had learned by this time really did help me make sense of some of my experiences. Most notably, as I will return to, Karl Marx and the later tradition of critical theory helped me understand economic domination both within the British class system and under capitalism more generally. I had also read much on the theory, science, and politics of mental health to try to understand my various distressing experiences. Yet while some of this was helpful to an extent, nothing I had come across fit neatly with the complex and messy forms of disablement that had structured my life since the beginning.

On the one hand, while I had found my autism diagnosis helpful, much about it was also distressing. The dominant medicalised narrative suggested that being autistic made me somehow tragic, broken, and in need of fixing. This narrative reinforced the constant messages I had received since school, indicating that there was something inherently wrong with me. Alternatively, popular critics of psychiatric diagnosis, from the anti-psychiatry tradition, suggested things like autism and depression were merely illusory 'labels' rather than real medical conditions. For them, people like me were not really disabled, but just experiencing normal day-to-day problems. These two binary options seemed to offer either disability shame or disability denial, neither of which was helpful. This was why I found discovering the neurodiversity movement, which offered a different analysis, so liberating. It was this that set me on the path to writing this book.

DISCOVERING NEURODIVERSITY

The neurodiversity movement began to emerge in autistic activist groups during the 1990s, back when I was still a child struggling to process in school. At that time, autism was widely seen as an individual medical tragedy, incompatible with living a good human life. The only hope for autistic people and our families, it was thought, was that we would one day be fixed through behavioural conditioning or biomedical intervention.

Yet by around 1993, the wider availability of personal computers and the internet meant that autistic people were able to begin connecting online for the first time. This meeting of autistic minds brought an intense period of consciousness-raising that would challenge the dominant understanding of autism. For once they were together, these pioneering autistic activists began to realise they all experienced similar problems, including the kinds I have just noted in my own life. In turn, they began to argue that perhaps the problems they all experienced had less to do with their brains being broken, and more to do with societal failure to accommodate their neurological differences. They thus started to argue for what one 1997 report from the *New York Times* described as a form of 'neurological pluralism'. This emphasised the need for the behaviours and processing styles of atypical people to be accepted and supported rather than framed as medical pathologies to be controlled, treated, and cured.

Out of this came the idea of *neurodiversity*, first documented by a sociology student called Judy Singer. The basic point was that we should reject the very idea of a 'normal' brain and of the 'neurotypical' as an ideal. Instead, it implied viewing mental functioning more in the way we view biodiversity. In this view, it takes all kinds of minds for society to function, and thus normality should not be assumed to be superior to divergence. Rather, there were many kinds of minds. Each was enabled or disabled in different environments, and no single one was naturally superior to all the others. The kind of sensory problems I myself had experienced, for instance, could be seen as caused by the neurotypical-biased design of schools, the workplace, and public spaces. More broadly, in this view, much autistic suffering – such as the bullying I had encountered at school – could be understood largely in the context of societal marginalisation and discrimination.

To remedy this, Singer and other activists thus called for a new 'politics of neurological diversity'. For them, this would consist in a new movement that would be modelled on the earlier civil rights movements that had sought to end racial, gendered, and sexual segregation and oppression within and across borders. This new neurodiversity movement would, they hoped, supplement existing struggles by fighting for the rights of the neurologically weird and disabled. The hope was to end neurodivergent oppression everywhere by redesigning the world in ways that would cultivate neurodivergent thriving.

This call for a politics of neurodiversity had a great impact, and many new advocates rallied to the cause. Yet while these early efforts had focused on autism, the framework and vocabularies that emerged from autistic spaces were quickly adopted by a great many others. First, this was among those with other developmental disabilities such as Attention Deficit Hyperactivity Disorder (ADHD) or dyspraxia. In turn, the neurodiversity framing began to be adopted by those with other diagnoses such as bipolar disorder and borderline personality disorder, not to mention those with no official diagnosis at all.

The breadth of this expansion is captured in Kassiane Asasumasu's coining of 'neurodivergent' in the early 2000s. For her, this refers to any kind of neurological functioning that is considered 'divergent from typical',[5] whether mere differences are disabled by an unaccommodated society or medical conditions such as epilepsy.

Asasumasu wrote that the concept was 'specifically a tool of inclusion', available for any neurologically atypical person who found it
useful. While this expansion raised questions about the scope and
limits of the neurodiversity framework, it was important as it helped
more people gather under the neurodiversity banner. At the same
time, as Steve Graby[6] has observed, while the anti-psychiatry proponents had emphasised that they were unlike people with bodily
disabilities – and that psychiatrised people were not *really* disabled
– the neurodiversity perspective embraced the disabled identity.
Emphasising the similarities between mental and bodily disablement allowed a broader, more inclusive politics, with neurodiversity
proponents straddling the divide between people with medicalised
bodies and those with medicalised minds.

As the movement grew, the theory of neurodiversity was further
developed to fit. Most notably, for me, by 2011, a young autistic
scholar called Nick Walker proposed that neurodivergent liberation required not just rights. It also required a mass scientific and
cultural paradigm shift. This shift would be away from the dominant
'pathology paradigm', which for Walker was defined by highly
restricted standards of mental normality and by the default pathologisation and stigmatisation of divergence. Walker drew attention
to this as she took it to underpin psychiatric and psychological
research and practice, as well as more general societal responses to
neurodivergence.

In its place, she argued, neurodiversity proponents must build
a 'neurodiversity paradigm', which would embrace and support
a much broader range of cognitive and emotional variation. This
prospect offered not just hope to countless neurodivergent people,
but also an ideal to collectively work towards. And this was an ideal
that, as a philosopher, I would soon dedicate my own efforts towards,
since I knew that shifting the paradigm would require more fundamental theoretical work alongside shifting scientific, clinical, and
cultural practices.

My own first exposure to this perspective was in 2012, one year
after Walker's seminal publication. For me, reading Singer, Walker,
and other proponents offered a different path to both the pathology

paradigm framing and to the anti-psychiatry denialists. What it did was allow me to fully recognise the reality of my disabilities, yet in a way that helped me develop an awareness of the political nature of the kinds of hardship that had structured my whole existence. Through the neurodiversity lens I began to wonder, for instance, whether since the very start, I had been disabled by a neuro-normative society. This, I came to see, had hindered my learning, my development, and my prospects right from the beginning of life. I also began to understand my trauma and mental illness as stemming from not just relative poverty and parental neglect but also a structurally ableist world. For me as for so many others, this more nuanced understanding felt liberating, allowing me to make sense of my life anew.

Just as important, this perspective also helped me develop solidarity with other disabled and chronically ill people, and even a sense of disability pride. Together, all this helped me combat isolation, political inertia, and shame. It also helped me, and so many others, begin to see a way out. It finally suddenly seemed possible for neurodivergent people to collectively change the world – to make it more inclusive for the neurologically weird and disabled. This provided a kind of hope that had never before seemed possible. As such, I threw myself into the movement just as it was beginning to grow rapidly, to an extent and in ways that nobody back then could have predicted.

THE LIMITS OF LIBERALISM

As the movement has grown since 2012, most neurodiversity activism has continued in a liberal, rights-based framework, which focuses on incremental reforms within the current system. Simultaneously there have been huge collective efforts focused on overcoming the pathology paradigm. Through my own period of involvement, I have contributed much time and effort to this dual approach. This was first through blogging and campaigning, next through doctoral research, and since then advocating, teaching, and researching in academia. Yet despite finding the neurodiversity perspective so useful, and despite contributing to efforts to develop this perspective myself, I also began to find the dominant approach to neurodiversity analysis, activism, and advocacy unsatisfying.

To be sure, I did clearly see first-hand how the liberal approach made important gains in a short time. Given continuous pressure from neurodivergent activists, research has increasingly drawn on neurodiversity theory, cultural representations of neurodivergence have become less stigmatising, and how we design our social world has likewise begun to change. In Britain, to give just a few examples, supermarkets and cinemas often have autism-friendly hours, more airports have sensory rooms for neurodivergent children, and classrooms and workplaces are making increased efforts to become more inclusive in line with new rights legislation.

And yet, over time I increasingly came to see that, despite its very real successes, the liberal, rights-based approach to neurodiversity activism also had significant limitations. Consider some of the following facts. Despite our combined efforts over many years, most research, policy, and practice remained based within the pathology paradigm. Even when it came to autism – where progress has been quickest – the most widely used autism 'therapy' was still Applied Behaviour Analysis. This was designed to use a system of punishments and rewards to try to make autistic children more 'normal'. Despite countless critiques from neurodiversity proponents who see this method as abusive and a form of conversion therapy, this multi-billion-pound international industry continued its growth, only making minor concessions to its critics.

At the same time, many experts in the old, medicalised paradigm began rebranding as 'neurodiversity' experts without significantly changing their approach. Psychiatrists, psychologists, and politicians were adopting the vocabularies of the neurodiversity movement – albeit often incorrectly – and making superficial changes to practice while leaving the logics of the pathology paradigm intact. Neurodiversity activists had referred to this co-option as 'neurodiversity-lite', indicating how it leaves the dominant paradigm and political order unchallenged despite the shift in presentation. Yet given their existing positions of power, it was these neurodiversity-lite proponents who were often given the biggest platforms, and who were positioned as exemplars of the neurodiversity approach.

More broadly, regardless of gains in rights and recognition, the apparatus of social forces that disenables and discriminates against neurodivergent people remained intact. Consider, to give just a few of countless potential examples, how around a quarter of prison inmates in the UK still had ADHD;[7] how people with intellectual disabilities were still routinely segregated in education and accommodation; or how autistic people in Denmark, purportedly among the happiest countries in the world, were still around three times more likely to die by suicide than members of the general population.[8]

None of this was 'natural'. Rather, it seemed to me, it must be determined by complex and deeper societal power relations, structures, and norms. As such, despite real gains in rights and representation, it was clear that the movement remained far from achieving its long-term goal of liberating neurodivergent people through shifting the paradigm more broadly. If anything, while liberal reformism did help some neurodivergent people, it was mainly those who were already relatively privileged in other ways – white, middle-class, and so on – while leaving multiply marginalised neurodivergents stuck in a variety of carceral systems, homeless, or in other unbearable situations. For me, all this raised the question of exactly what it would take to achieve emancipation, and why gains in rights and recognition had not led to this. It also raised the question of exactly where the pathology paradigm had come from, why it had been able to become so dominant, and how it related to the broader economic and systemic factors that I increasingly saw it as so deeply intertwined with.

Through my historical research into the origins of the pathology paradigm, I became more convinced that the problem lay at a deeper level, relating more specifically to underlying social, technological, and economic factors. Because so many of the failures of liberal activism also related to broader economic factors, I began to turn to different frameworks to make sense of the workings of the pathology paradigm. This led me back to an older, more radical tradition that emphasised the role of political economy in social domination. This was the Marxian tradition, as opposed to the liberal political position most neurodiversity advocacy has sat within.

This tradition itself was not new to me. Especially given my own experience of poverty and homelessness when young – not to mention poorly paid, precarious work, insecure housing, and much else as an adult – I had long found Marxian analyses of class domination illuminating. And just as a Marxian approach had, since Marx's time, been further developed in a number of new ways, I suspected it would be useful to develop a similar analysis for neurodiversity. This would be to help position neurodivergent oppression within the broader economic system that had come to dominate the world over the prior centuries, and in turn to help develop a politics of neurodiversity to help resist this.

Initially, I struggled with this project, not least since many fundamental commitments of Marxism seemed at odds with the standard liberal neurodiversity approach. I also disliked most Marxian analyses of mental health, since they were grounded more in the anti-psychiatry tradition that I had come to see as reactionary and outdated. Yet as I slowly pieced together such an analysis, drawing on not just Marx but a range of later scholars in the broader Marxian tradition, I increasingly came to see this approach as providing a deeper understanding of neurodivergent disablement and oppression than I had hitherto held. In the end I began to think of this approach as *Neurodivergent Marxism*. And I came to see this as distinct from, and a challenge to, both liberal neurodiversity and orthodox Marxism.

NEURODIVERSITY AND MARXISM

To clarify Neurodivergent Marxism, as I understand it, it will help to say a bit about Marx's critique of capitalist domination. At base, this was developed through Marx's theory of what has been called 'historical' or 'dialectical' materialism.[9] This frames our consciousness, thought, and perception, as significantly constrained by the broader material and economic conditions of the age. In turn, it seeks to navigate the prospects for change in the contradictions that arise from the clash between agency and historical forces. In Marx's own words, humans 'make their own history, but they do not make it just as they please; they do not make it under circumstances chosen by themselves, but under circumstances directly encountered, given and transmitted from the past'.[10] Vitally, it was this way of viewing history that allowed Marx to develop his historical analysis of capitalism.

Living through the nineteenth century as England was swiftly industrialising, Marx identified capitalism as a system where only a small part of the population owns the means of production, while most of the population is mined for productivity, with capitalists extracting surplus value from their wage-labour. Whereas domination and inequality were previously based on the more direct and violent political power of kings, lords, and so on, in this new system technically free workers were primarily compelled by economic relations. In this, capitalism stratified new classes of people – most notably the bourgeoisie, the workers, and the unemployed surplus – distinguished by objective material relations and positionings within the broader global system.

Through his historical analysis of capitalism, he came to see this system as bringing both unique benefits and problems when compared to previous economic systems. On the one hand, he saw that its benefits included helping end the more brutal forms of oppression of the feudal era, while simultaneously bringing increased technological progress and greater levels of productivity that had the potential to greatly benefit the population at large. Yet Marx also saw capitalism as containing inherent contradictions that necessitated deep-seated inequality and constant economic crisis.

Perhaps the most important contradiction, for our purposes, was grounded in his concept of alienation. For Marx, humans are essentially social animals who use our creative potentials for artistic and innovative projects, and our 'productive forces' to make the world more habitable for us. Put more concretely, while there is no fixed 'human nature', we are at least relatively unique in making tools, building houses, growing crops, painting, writing music, and so forth, in ways that can help us develop, thrive, and prosper.[11] This was important for Marx because, if we must use our creative and productive forces not for our individual or collective good, but rather for others to profit, our freedom and developmental potentials are thus simultaneously expanded yet stifled. While some alienation had always existed, since capitalism typically brought longer working hours, heightened divisions of labour, and more gruelling, monotonous work than the feudal age, Marx saw this newer system as leading to increased alienation. This was from our own creative potentials, from the products of our labour, and ultimately from each other, making every aspect of our existence increasingly alienated as the domain and power of capitalism grew.

Given this, for Marx, while capitalism did bring greater productive capacity, including for medical technology and support, at a deeper level it was simultaneously harmful to both bodily and mental health. For under capitalism, most of the population are workers who have little control over our prospects. We are effectively forced to constantly use our productive forces, and debilitate our bodies and minds, in the service of capitalists, just to earn enough to survive. In this context, good health becomes ever harder to maintain, even with the many benefits that capitalism brings.

Looked at this way, for Marx, a key contradiction of capitalism is that, under the 'mute compulsion' of capitalist economic power, wealth is produced collectively by the many, who are forced to sell wage-labour to be exploited and alienated. Yet this wealth is then appropriated privately by the few at the expense of the many. It is this contradiction that Marx thought might bring the conflicts that would one day end capitalism, allowing a shift towards a freer, more equal society. Following this, he hoped, such deeply ingrained divisions in social class would be consigned to history.

While Marx was born in 1818, over two centuries ago, the core of this analysis is no less relevant today. For despite increases in living standards in some times and places, worsening crises continue to send shocks through the global economy, and such inequalities remain deeply entrenched. It is not just that, as my own experience attests, many of us still live in relative poverty even in the wealthiest nations. It is also that globally, as one recent report found, since 1995, the richest 1 per cent have accumulated nearly 20 times more wealth than the poorest 50 per cent.[12]

It is important to note here that Marx's analysis has been updated and expanded since his death in 1883, and early orthodox readings of his works have been challenged. Most notably, the rather crass and distorted understanding of Marxism wrongly used to justify Stalinist totalitarianism was hotly contested by Marxist humanists[13] and Frankfurt School critical theorists,[14] who emphasised that Marx was arguing for a freer society rather than one that was state-controlled. In turn, scholars in the Black Radical tradition have shown how primary racism and colonialism were to the emergence of capitalism as a global system,[15] feminist scholarship has examined the ways in which capital continuously extracts unpaid emotional and reproductive work from women,[16] disability studies scholars have examined how capitalism disabled us and worsens disability discrimination,[17] and environmental scholars and activists have since emphasised how capital will literally destroy our planet and end all human life if it is not stopped.[18] All of these accounts update and supplement Marx's analysis, which had focused primarily on the white, male worker in Europe.

Neurodivergent Marxism continues in this updated Marxian tradition. While my understanding is heavily grounded in and synthesises aspects of this broader Marxian tradition, I go beyond them by providing the first history and politics of neurodiversity from a Marxian perspective. In this, I show how the rise and workings of the pathology paradigm are intimately intertwined with not just the vested interests of various groups or people, but, vitally, the underlying logics of capitalism itself. This thus begins with covering how our current scientific and cultural understandings of neurological disability and normality grew in relation to specific economic conditions, power relations, and ideological landscapes. This then develops into a materialist history of the pathology paradigm, tracing how its ideas arose from and in turn functioned to naturalise the shifting material relations of capitalism as it continually develops.

In doing this, I also clarify how and why capitalism is so intensely neuronormative, becoming more so with each passing decade. While all societies and economic systems have some standard of what is considered acceptable or valuable mental functioning – and while some mental illness and disability will always exist – I suggest capitalism is disposed to much tighter standards than other modes of production. In this view, neurodivergent oppression and disablement is established as a feature of the system rather than a bug. And in turn, since the pathology paradigm is a product of the broader economic system, overcoming it will require more than a revolution in how we think about neurodiversity. It will also require changing much deeper structures in our society, in ways that are usually left unclarified in existing neurodiversity theory.

While a materialist analysis helps account for restricting neuronormativity, an updated analysis of alienation simultaneously allows us to make sense of rising rates of mental health problems in recent decades. In particular, I am concerned with seemingly rising depression, anxiety, and trauma even in the otherwise neurotypical population. While the kind of alienation Marx detailed in industrial England still remains, it is my contention that as capitalism has intensified, the kind of alienation we experience has shifted. More specifically, many workers today perform cognitive, attentive, and emotional labour more than the manual labour of Marx's time, while our requirements as consumers and citizens, to have the correct desires, have also been restricted. All this, as we will see, contributes both to tightening neuronormativity, and thus increased disablement, but also to much more widespread mental health problems even for those who fall within the neurological norms of the age.

The implication of this is that, increasingly, new forms of domination often have less to do with social class, which now, to an extent, is more fluid than in the nineteenth century, and much more to do with where each of us falls on the new cognitive hierarchies of capitalism. Of course, this is not to minimise the ongoing significance of class domination, let alone the importance of other intersections. Rather, it is to show how even when traditional forms of domination do lessen to even some small extent, they are merely replaced with increased neuronormative domination instead. Hence a further contradiction of capitalism, for me, is that even when class mobility increases to some extent, a different kind of domination, this time regarding neurodiversity, arises in equal measure. It is in this contradiction, that I take to become more salient as capitalism further intensifies, that I see a key site of struggle, and perhaps emancipation, in the twenty-first century.

THE EMPIRE OF NORMALITY

This is the first book that provides a history of capitalism that places neurodiversity, rather than class, at its centre. While I do take an intersectional approach that considers class, race, gender, sexuality, and bodily disability, my focus on neurodiversity allows me to trace the emergence of what I call the Empire of Normality. This refers to an apparatus of material relations, social practices, scientific research programmes, bureaucratic mechanisms, economic compulsions, and administrative procedures that emerge from fundamental dispositions of the capitalist system, at least once it reaches a certain stage of development. Together, these bring a much more restricted bodily, cognitive, and emotional normal range than those seen in any previous society. Simultaneously, the framing of this as an empire helps me to emphasise the connection between neurodivergent oppression, colonialism, and imperialism. This in turn should allow us to examine the prospects for developing a politics of neurodiversity that equally helps work towards collective liberation.

For my alternative telling, rather than attempting to provide a comprehensive history, I focus on carefully chosen key thinkers positioned in their broader material context. My aim with this is not to resurrect them as 'great' (or not so great) men, but rather to show how the progression of pathology paradigm thinking, especially at key moments, has been significantly determined by material factors in ways that are both guided by and reify capitalist power relations and hierarchies. This allows us to see how the material and the ideological continually interact and mutually reinforce each other even, perhaps especially, through the work of those usually positioned as having helped science progress.

With this in mind, I begin by covering the work of the ancient Greek Hippocratic doctors as well as other ancient medical approaches across the globe. These tended to view health as a form of harmony or balance, either within the individual or between individual and environment. This only ended, as we will see, with the rise of capitalism, specifically given its emphasis on competition and worker productivity. This new economic system led humans to be reinterpreted as machines, which I explore through the thought of the philosopher Descartes. And in turn it led to the concept of 'normality' arising and being utilised to reimagine the nature of health and ability. This, I show, then began being used to rank and control populations in ways that, while bringing scientific progress, nonetheless became increasingly oppressive. In time, the idea of normality entered so deeply into our collective consciousness, it began to seem timeless and objective, thus obscuring its material genesis and contingency.

Within this context, I trace the pathology paradigm proper in large part to the work of a strange and pioneering scientist called Francis Galton – the half-cousin of Charles Darwin, known today for being the founder of eugenics as well as of many scientific innovations. For our purposes, the most significant thing Galton introduced in the late nineteenth century was a novel way of comparing cognition and measuring biology, which grounded a Darwinian ranking system that naturalised the cognitive hierarchies of industrial capitalism as well as its hierarchies of class, race, and gender. The point of this for Galton was to formalise and amplify the normalising and control of populations, now legitimised as a scientific pursuit. And part of the effect of this was an increased conceptual blending and conflation of normality, productivity, and health.

A key part of my argument is that this paradigm was then taken up and expanded, with great fervour, by influential psychiatrists such as Emil Kraepelin as well as in psychological, psychometric, and biomedical research. In tracing Galton's influence, I thus cover how a broader eugenic ideology became culturally hegemonic, while his research paradigm simultaneously allowed the cognitive hierarchies of advanced capitalism to become reified through guiding the assumptions, methods, and results of scientific knowledge production. I thus position Galton – rather than Kraepelin, as is typical in histories of psychiatry – as the founder of the currently dominant scientific paradigm used in psychiatry and related fields.

This shines a light on how the ideological biases determined by the material relations of capitalism and imperial Britain – channelled through Galton – have since guided scientific knowledge production, public understanding, policy, and clinical practice relating to neurodiversity to this very day. This has been so even while the old imperial order has crumbled in other important ways. It is this new apparatus of scientific, administrative, cultural, and legal impositions that constitute the Empire of Normality. Long after the British Empire has crumbled, I show, many of its hierarchies and power relations have been maintained, reproduced, and expanded through this apparatus, which has not only survived but grown ever-more hegemonic as capitalism has continued to intensify. Thus, for me, the key problem is not the pathology paradigm alone, but how capitalist logics and the pathology paradigm mutually reinforce each other, leaving no possibility of neurodivergent liberation without deep systemic change.

My aim is not to develop a set of policy proposals or a political strategy. Rather, it is to help clarify an underlying problem that I see as a deeper, older, and more insidious than the pathology paradigm. Clarifying this problem is just the first step towards what will need to be a much more prolonged, collective effort to combat the Empire of Normality, that is, the apparatus that sits behind and necessitates the pathology paradigm. Only by understanding how the paradigm relates to this broader apparatus and in turn to fundamental dispositions of the capitalist mode of production will we be able to clearly comprehend what neurodivergent liberation would require.

It is worth emphasising that I also write with some urgency for the current political moment. In the past few years, as recognition and influence of neurodivergent activism has rapidly increased, it is not just that the vocabularies, concepts, and suggestions of neurodiversity proponents have begun being co-opted by clinicians and politicians to maintain the status quo. It is also that countless new diversity and inclusion consultants increasingly charge large sums of money to speak to businesses who then come to see neurodivergent people as new resources to be mined for productivity. In this, we see the rise of what I call neuro-Thatcherism, in which capitalism even subverts attempts to resist its harmful effects, turning these attempts back into new opportunities for the maximisation of profit and productivity. In this, the liberatory potential of this new movement is being stifled just as the movement seems to be gaining power.

At the same time, the anti-psychiatry movement, which waned towards the end of the twentieth century, is now growing in popularity again. In contrast to my analysis, this tradition sees psychiatry itself, and belief in the concept of 'mental illness', as the core problem. Although not all anti-psychiatrists took this position, this approach, which stems from the work of the right-wing libertarian Thomas Szasz, has perhaps been the most influential in offering an alternative story to mainstream psychiatry.

Importantly, while my analysis may have some superficial overlap with Szasz, I wholly resist the idea that this means the various things we currently call autism, ADHD, or so forth are not 'real' disabilities. I also forcefully resist the Szaszian claim that mental illness is a 'myth'. While I do critique the foundations and effects of the dominant psychiatric paradigm, my critique is of how the concept of health has been conflated with normality and productivity, and of how disablement and illness have actually increased, under the material relations of capitalism. It is not a rejection of recognising mental illness or disability as such. Indeed, as we will see, I argue that anti-psychiatry is part of the problem, not the solution. For despite looking different on the surface, in fact, it reinforces rather than challenges the logics of the pathology paradigm and the broader apparatus of normality.

By contrast, in tracing the rise of the neurodiversity movement, I synthesise the work of seminal neurodiversity theorists Judy Singer and Nick Walker with my Marxian approach. This is important as it allows me to clarify as-yet unidentified contradictions of capitalism that show the futility of neuro-Thatcherism. The most important of these regards a tendency towards a neuronormative double-bind that increasingly traps each of us, regardless of whether we are closer or further from the neurotypical ideal. Those aspects of our species-wide neuro-cognitive diversity that it cannot currently use are disenabled, devalued, and discriminated against; while those it can use are ruthlessly exploited and thus made unwell. Either way, I argue, all human minds and selves are estranged from one another through the psychic hierarchies this produces. This leads to a situation where we all become sick or disabled, or at the very least where wellbeing is elusive for most of us. On this view, then, it is not the neurotypical who oppresses the neurodivergent, but capitalist domination that, in a certain sense, creates and harms both neurotypicals and neurodivergents, albeit in slightly different ways depending on any given individual's proximity to the norm.

Indeed, as already alluded to, part of what I seek to show is that while capitalist societies have allowed some degree of mobility regarding social class, this has only meant that domination shifts more towards neurodivergence rather than diminishing overall. This, I argue, undermines the last promise of capitalism, which purports to help us approach a meritocracy where free individuals are valued not by their inherited status but by their virtues and how hard they work.

It is not just that this is untrue at the national level, where class still significantly constrains individual economic outcomes, or at the global level, since the wealth of the Global North precisely relies on the relative poverty of the global south. It is also, I argue, that even where capitalism does bring limited advances that allow increased mobility in social class, we simply switch more traditional forms of domination for neuronormative domination relative to the increasingly intense cognitive needs of capital. Thus, there seems to be only a very limited possibility of liberation under capitalism, and only an offer of different forms of domination and alienation depending on where we are positioned. It is this, I argue, that grounds the need for a more radical politics of neurodiversity, directed against the Empire of Normality itself.

1
Rise of the machines

The most important parts of our story take place since the early nineteenth century, but it is helpful to begin with a more sweeping account that provides some broader context. Most significantly, this regards how the shift from feudalism to capitalism brought a fundamental change in how health was conceptualised.

The chapter begins by briefly looking at how health was understood as a form of harmony in Ancient Greece and elsewhere in the ancient world. This persisted until at least the seventeenth century. We then turn to the French philosopher René Descartes, whose work I take as symbolic of a broader shift in Enlightenment thinking about the body and health. For Descartes, the body was reconceptualised as a machine. In this view, health was no longer a matter of harmony, but rather a mechanistic matter of working properly. Finally, I turn to the rise of capitalism and the Industrial Revolution. I show that, far from being an inevitable scientific development, the reimagining of the body as a machine became so broadly embraced because it helped naturalise new hierarchies that emerged from capitalism itself. This overview, illustrating how capitalism brought with it a new conception and correlating science of health, will help set the stage for the following chapters on the rise of the pathology paradigm.

HEALTH AS HARMONY

The time of the Hippocratics was the classical world of the Greek city-states where famous battles were fought, the great poets composed their epics, and Socrates argued with his fellow citizens in the marketplace of Athens. Because medicine was so basic, chronic illness and disability were widely incorporated into daily life, and there was nothing like the systemic disability segregation that came later. Archaeological evidence shows that temples, for instance, had ramps to aid access for those with impaired mobility.[1] Nonetheless, there was still discrimination against disabled people. Most notably, in this context, it was widely held that illness was a punishment – or, sometimes, gift – from the gods. This 'moral model' of disability dates at least back to Ancient Egypt, where healing was administered by sorcerer-medics who would banish evil spirits alongside providing basic medical intervention.

Hippocrates himself was born around 460 BC on the Island of Kos, off the coast of Turkey. He was first taught by his father, a medic called Heraclides. After learning all Heraclides had to teach, Hippocrates travelled widely to learn more about medicine. While little is known for certain about his travels or later life, we do know from his contemporary Plato that Hippocrates returned to Kos and became famous for his medical work and teachings even in his own time.[2]

We also know that a great many texts, known together as the *Hippocratic Corpus*, still survive. These were written either by Hippocrates or his followers. And from these the legacy of the Hippocratic tradition becomes clear. For while illness had traditionally been viewed through a religious lens, the Hippocratics came to understand illness naturalistically, as problems of the body or mind. They also pioneered methods of observation and record-keeping, and they came to develop complex diagnostic systems for interpreting and treating illness.

In time those working in this tradition were able to treat infected wounds, build an understanding of the importance of nutrition, and to develop important surgical tools and interventions. They also saw the brain, in the words of one Hippocratic text, as 'the seat of madness and delirium, of the fears and frights which assail us'.[3] When it came to neurological disorder, they distinguished between mania, melancholy, insanity, and epilepsy, in ways not too different to the distinctions found in the works of early psychiatrists over two millennia later.[4] It is thus here that we first see the recognition of specific neurological conditions as opposed to the idea that madness was inflicted by mischievous or wrathful gods.

Yet this is where the similarities with contemporary medicine end. The most important difference is that their understanding of health was wholly unlike those developed later. For today, disability and disorder are understood in relation to concepts of statistical or medical *normality*. Yet in fact, there was no such conception in the ancient world. While the Pythagoreans had developed the concept of the arithmetic 'mean' shortly prior to the birth of Hippocrates, this concept was highly abstract. As Simon Raper has written, the 'Pythagoreans mention the arithmetic mean in the context of music and proportion, along with the geometric and harmonic means, but there is no suggestion of using it for summarising data'.[5] Thus, the idea of 'normal' functioning – or more concretely, of the normal heart rate, normal lung capacity, normal height, normal cognitive ability, and so forth – would have been wholly alien to the medics of antiquity.

Instead, illness was defined as a disruption of bodily harmony, balance, or equilibrium. For the Hippocratics, the balance of health was primarily between what they saw as the four primary properties or 'humours' of blood, phlegm, yellow bile, and black bile. On this view, as the historian Andrew Scull summarises, 'each of us is composed of four basic elements which contend for superiority' in ways that can lead to them being more or less balanced.[6] If these were in balance then the body was healthy, and different illnesses were produced by different forms of imbalance.

Equally, the health as harmony could be between individual and environment. For instance, the dominance of different humours was associated with different seasons, which tended to bring different illnesses. Similarly, the Hippocratics also suggested neurological functioning could be affected by things such as changes in the weather. For instance, as one Hippocratic text posits, a 'southerly wind' could 'relax the brain' and its blood vessels, while a northerly wind would 'solidify' parts of the brain, with each of these bringing different cognitive effects.[7] If someone was ill, this was taken as a sign that there was a lack of harmony in humours or between individual and environment, and different forms of imbalance were taken to explain different medical problems.

While our focus here will be on Western conceptions of health, it is remarkable to consider that equilibrium conceptions of bodily and mental health can also be seen in a range of traditional medical philosophies globally. These include the Ayurvedic tradition in India, Ancient Chinese medicine, Ancient Egyptian medicine, and Incan oral medical traditions.[8] To be sure, each of these did differ in an array of complexities and nuances, and none used the Hippocratic concept of 'humours'. Yet they and many other approaches did see health as, in one sense or another, a matter of harmony or equilibrium. This was either within the individual, or between individual and either the environment or their community. For instance, as Alexus McLeod summarises, those in the ancient Confucian tradition in China believed that if 'we are in bad, vicious or unhealthy communities, our beliefs, emotions, expectations and attitudes (among other things) will be disordered in critical ways'.[9]

And so it was that across the ancient world, to be ill was not to have a mechanical abnormality, but to be out of balance with aspects of self, others, or environment. And far from being confined to antiquity, these traditions continued until quite recently. The humoral tradition, for instance, continued to be developed in Ancient Rome through the work of Galen, during the Islamic Golden Age by Ibn Sina, and then throughout medieval Europe. Likewise, other ancient equilibrium traditions globally continued until the modern age. Across the world the underlying equation between health and harmony, illness and imbalance, was to remain dominant until colonialism, the Enlightenment and, most of all, the rise of capitalism.

THE BODY AS MACHINE

In part the shift to a new way of understanding health concerned the new concept of 'normality', which I will return to in the following chapter. But it also concerned the new mechanistic understanding of the body. While there were certainly hints of this earlier, the machine metaphor was most fully and memorably proposed in the seventeenth century by the French philosopher René Descartes. Born in France in 1596 and later travelling and studying throughout Europe, Descartes developed his insights just as the Enlightenment was dawning. Over this period, a renewed focus on reason and observation, and the breaking of traditional dogmas, would bring huge advances in European philosophy, science, and technology.

While his interest in medicine arose earlier and was built on the work of his contemporaries, Descartes' own pathbreaking work followed the death of his 5-year-old daughter Francine. Tragically, Francine had succumbed to scarlet fever in 1640, leaving Descartes deeply stricken. This seems to have led him to turn towards more universal themes such as the nature of the soul alongside the workings of the body. It is quite feasible that Francine's tragic death influenced the suggestion he is best known for today. This was of a sharp dualism between the body and mind, whereby the mind could survive the decline of the mechanistic body, or even death itself.

It was in his 1641 book *Meditations*, written in the Netherlands shortly after Francine's death, that Descartes outlined his understanding of the body. In particular, he suggested a number of memorable analogies between body and machine. For instance, he likened the healthy or sick body to a well-made or broken clock. He also made analogies between specific body-parts and specific machines or devices, likening the eyes, for instance, to telescopes. In this way, he wrote, we can ultimately consider 'the body of a human being as a kind of machine made up of bones, nerves, muscles, veins, blood, and skin'.[10] While his conception of the mind was more abstract and compatible with there being an immortal soul, his conception of body was wholly confined to what could be seen and studied objectively.

In suggesting this, Descartes was rejecting the traditional vision of the body as a dynamic organism, made up of competing humours, and always positioned in relation to different environments. Instead, for him, it was now a complex machine made up of smaller mechanistic parts that worked together to maintain health. As such, either specific parts of the body, or one's overall bodily functioning, could be working or broken, and in turn fixed, by anyone with sufficient knowledge and resources – much like the clocks or other machines made or repaired by the great tradesmen of Descartes' time.

What was so radical about this reimagining was that, in contrast to his own experience with Francine, it allowed the hope that there might come a day when any human body would be able to be fixed. And in retrospect we can see that Descartes' hope was not unfounded. Today, scarlet fever is easily treatable with antibiotics, as are many other diseases that would have been fatal in Descartes' time. The rise of a mechanistic medicine surely has thus saved countless others from suffering the kind of grief that Descartes held.

Yet initially Descartes's comparisons, due to prevailing religious sensibilities, were considered utterly outrageous. At the time he was writing, most doctors were still working in the humoral tradition. But by then medical thought and practice had become deeply intertwined with the dominant Christian belief system. In practice, doctors routinely relied on astrological analysis of star signs for interpretations of specific illnesses or choosing treatments. These same doctors saw new scientific approaches to medicine as a threat to not just their medical authority but also their religious worldview. Indeed, in 1643, two years after publishing his *Meditations*, Descartes himself was forced to flee as his philosophy was condemned as heretical.

Descartes did not live to see society embrace a mechanistic understanding of the body. He died in 1650, seemingly after being poisoned with arsenic by a Catholic priest in Sweden.[11] Unsurprisingly, Descartes' views remained relatively marginalised through the following century. But by the turn of the nineteenth century, it was increasingly hard to deny that the humoral approach was not just outdated, but often used to justify bizarre and unhelpful treatments. In the early eighteenth century, for instance, there had been a revival in the ancient practice of leeching, where leeches were used to suck blood from the bodies of patients to restore their humoral balance. Indeed, even as late as the early 1850s, Manchester Royal Infirmary used around 50,000 leeches a year, regardless of the lack of benefit this brought patients.[12]

By contrast, the more mechanistic understanding of the body would, as it became increasingly dominant in the latter half of the nineteenth century, come to pave the way for modern medicine to emerge. It would be here that our contemporary understanding not just of bodily anatomy and functioning, but also of germs, bacteria, viruses, and much else would begin to be developed. The Cartesian approach to the body thus helped bring a revolution in the science of medicine.

And yet despite significantly improving our understanding, the shift to the individual machine metaphor was not an inevitable and inescapable product of scientific progress. Like other metaphors used in science, it was equally a product of the historical, ideological, and technological context in which it took hold. To understand this, we need to turn to broader material and social factors that had already begun when Francine died – most importantly, the rise of the capitalist economic system.

THE TRIUMPH OF CAPITALISM

Such a wholesale embrace of the initially outrageous machine metaphor in the nineteenth century was made possible by the shift from feudal society, through merchant capitalism, to industrial capitalism. For by the time Descartes and his contemporaries were busy theorising about the body and mind, things had already changed much. Both international domination and commerce had already been rapidly developing in ways that were growing into a new world system. This would go on to develop in ways that would allow Descartes' initially outrageous proposal to become universally accepted across the capitalist world.

To clarify this, let us start with feudalism, the economic system that flourished from roughly the ninth to fifteenth centuries. In Europe, this had developed out of the breakdown of the Roman Empire, whose growth had relied heavily on slavery. But by the fourth century, due to successive slave revolts, landlords were forced to begin giving former slaves their own land to live on with their families. At the same time, free agricultural workers increasingly needed to turn to local lords for protection, but in doing so were required to swear fealty. While slavery did still exist, in many cases both former slaves and former free workers increasingly became peasants, or serfs. They would typically be able to live and work on their own land, and have access to 'common' forests, meadows, and lakes, while also having duties towards the lord in exchange for protection.

Beyond Europe, while the specifics were always different, we find other complex economic systems with feudal relations and pre-industrial production methods. For instance, across Africa there were a variety of complex feudalist forms of organisation based around the production of plantain bananas, cattle, and a variety of different goods. These had many similarities with European feudalism despite their religious and cultural differences. There had also been a feudal system in China that began to decline during the Ming period, which brought greater bureaucracy and central control.

In this economic system populations were small and production levels were low. Most people worked from their homes or on their land, producing little more than was needed to survive. Rather than having set deadlines or quotas, they tended to work together as family units producing whatever was necessary for self-sustenance. In this context, impairment and chronic illness were more accommodated in daily life. And this was not just as medical technology was so limited, or that there were very few hospitals, which then were more just refuges for people with leprosy. It was also that the workplace had been slower, more flexible, and more self-determined. Peasants worked fewer hours and had longer breaks than those working following the Industrial Revolution. Moreover, families and communities had often worked from home and as a unit, allowing a more flexible division of labour.

When it comes to disability, this is important because it meant that people with a wider range of impairments could be – and indeed, would often have to have been – included within broader family units or communities. A deaf or blind grandmother, for instance, may have still been able to weave or cook, a man with a cognitive disability may have laboured in the fields or helped in manufacturing, and people with mobility impairments could still work from home. More generally, in this period, as people still worked more with local communities and in relation to the seasons, it made sense to think of health as harmony between these various factors. And this includes the harmony of communities, which required an acceptance of a wider range of ways of functioning than were accepted in the industrial era.

All this began to change with the rise of capitalism. In part, the shift to capitalism emerged in the context of feudalist conceptions of property, which became gradually formalised as commerce developed across a more globalised market. In this period, states increasingly needed to quantify people and their assets to collect taxes, especially following conflicts between peasants and lords that allowed more peasants to own their own land and grow their own food. In Europe, for instance, following the Black Death, wiping out up to a third of the population in the thirteenth century, workers were also able to demand better conditions, and often rebelled in demand of these. In time, this allowed some landowners to begin making high profits from selling their products, and to begin accumulating wealth that could be reinvested.

New market economies and increases in commerce can be found across the world, from Italy to China, from around the sixteenth century. Increased specialisation of labour allowed for greater production and thus a boom in population. In turn, all this required stricter forms of measurement and quantification from the state, leading to the formalisation of surnames and standard measurements for assessing harvests and profits as the population grew. Classifications relating to ability were also increasingly formalised, leading to distinctions between the 'deserving' and 'undeserving' poor. The Elizabethan Poor Law of 1601, for instance, declared that 'Sums of Money' for the relief of the 'Lame, Impotent, Old, or Blind' should be provided by the parish, while the able-bodied poor should be set to work in industry.[13]

Across Europe, new economic relations were further driven by the way Europeans began to colonise parts of Africa from the twelfth century, and later the Americas. Having already developed early racialised notions about the Irish and Slavs, European colonisers adapted these notions to justify their subsequent genocide and enslavement of Black and Indigenous peoples.[14] This brought a new slave trade that was, if anything, much more brutal than the slavery of the Roman era. Out of this a larger, global capitalist system began to grow, with European nations, merchants, and explorers competing to colonise, murder, enslave, or trade with members of different communities across the globe. It was in this context that the Industrial Revolution would occur, making the conditions just right for Descartes' proposal to finally begin being more widely embraced.

THE PRODUCTIVE BODY

With this new power and the continued growth of commerce, new scientific and technological innovations were able to be developed in Europe. Interestingly, by the time Descartes proposed his mechanistic understanding of the body, there were already several workshops in Europe developing automata, where skilled workers developed expensive, self-operating machines. According to one tale, following the death of his daughter, 'a distraught Descartes had a clockwork Francine made: a walking, talking simulacrum'.[15] Yet while earlier automata may have inspired Descartes's philosophical breakthrough, it was later technological innovations that allowed it to become widely accepted.

The first steam pump, for instance, was developed in 1698 and the first steam engine in 1712. The spinning jenny, which allowed workers to produce multiple spools of thread simultaneously, was developed in 1764, and was followed by the spinning mule and the power loom in subsequent decades. Such inventions eased processes of production and could thus be invested in to generate profit. This in turn made an even greater demand for slave labour, to produce materials such as cotton not to mention goods such as tobacco, sugar, and tea. Specialisations in divisions of labour increased further still, allowing for ever greater levels of productivity and ever higher profits.

As merchant capitalism shifted to industrial capitalism, an ever-more powerful class of people, the bourgeoisie or capitalist class, came to rival the old powers of lords and kings. Because the bourgeoisie (by definition) owned the means of production, they could thus invest their profits and accumulate more and more capital. This small class thus became much more wealthy and influential. Everyone else, except an increasingly obsolete number of aristocrats, was either a free worker who sold their labour, an enslaved labourer forced to work, or was unemployed and thus part of a new surplus population. The work of women was also increasingly unrecognised, since they typically still worked at home while men went out to labour. For as reproductive and domestic work was not waged, it was no longer conceptualised as real work.[16] This ever-more dominant system thus broke apart traditional communities and restructured populations as per their place in its new economic hierarchies at national and international levels.

When it came to health, the effects of industrial capitalism were profound. It was not just, as Marx noted, that this system and its labour relations 'squanders human beings, living labour, more readily than does any other mode of production, squandering not only flesh and blood, but nerves and brain as well'.[17] Nor was it just that the living conditions of workers, packed into the squalor and pollution of industrial cities, brought new epidemics and diseases. While this was the case, what I want to stress is that in an important sense, it was capitalism that allowed the body itself to go from being understood as a dynamic organism to being a working or broken machine. And it was not just the fact that new machines were increasingly part of daily life, making it seem natural to use machines as metaphors for the sciences of the age. It was also that the mode of production itself favoured a reduction of people to living machines, since they were seen as working or broken in relation to their productive potential.

Most notably, in industrial England, as Vic Finkelstein has argued, as the new machines and workdays were increasingly standardised, the ideal worker was likewise standardised. Workers increasingly needed to be mobile enough to be able to travel to the factory. And they then needed to be able to work in line with the pace and production norms of the industrial workplace. At the same time, increased production of food meant that the population was able to expand. In this context, there were more and more surplus members of the workforce who had to compete against each other to gain employment. English factory workers could not, as Finkelstein writes, 'have any impairment which would prevent him or her from operating the machine. It was, therefore, the economic necessity of producing efficient machines for large-scale production that established able-bodiedness as the norm' in industrial England.[18]

This is not to say that disability was wholly synonymous with being unable to work in factories. In their study of disabled British coal miners in industrial England, historians Turner and Blackie stress how the 'dynamics of inclusion and exclusion' change 'within particular cohorts or occupations, and in different settings'.[19] In the case of coalmining, more disabled people, while encountering specific barriers and forms of discrimination, were included within the workforce. In this we see the emergence of a more general pattern, whereby disabled people and other members of the surplus class were sometimes included, if and when they are needed or can be exploited for profit. We also see how there is some fluidity between the working and surplus class, with members of either one moving into the other depending on the shifting needs of capital.

We also see a more complicated situation for Black slaves. Slaves were sold on slave markets and thus their bodies and minds were commodified in ways that paid labourers were not subjected to. As Stefanie Hunt-Kennedy has detailed, since they were not paid, plantation slaves were more often required to work even despite many being disabled – which they often were due to sustaining injuries following horrific abuse at the hands of slavers. Moreover, the 'worth' of enslaved labourers was determined by their 'resale value on the open market, as well as their individual output as workers'.[20] Because of how racism was built into the origins of capitalism, millions of enslaved labourers were thus doubly objectified in a way that was far worse than the already bad exploitation of white workers in Europe.

Indeed, as the research of Caitlin Rosenthal shows, it was plantation owners in the American South that pioneered the scientific management of enslaved workers. They did this, she writes, by paying 'close attention to how efficiently enslaved men and women picked cotton, frequently experimenting with new methods for maximizing output' recording and analysing 'data diligently and precisely, keeping accounts and comparing them year after year'.[21] In this, enslaved labourers were the first to be scientifically studied and manipulated to increase individual worker productivity in the service of capital. It was this kind of scientific management that paved the way for those methods that would later be expanded to all workers after the slave trade, and later slavery, were finally outlawed.

While conditions thus depended on context, what is clear is that throughout the capitalist world, the body itself, including the brain, increasingly came to be judged as being working or broken *in relation to* the individual's real or perceived productivity. And everyone's output was increasingly compared with everyone else's due to them being in competition with each other. In turn, individual productivity was increasingly observed, documented, classified, and assessed.

Through this period, worries regarding malingerers – people who were pretending to be ill to avoid work – continued to increase. Governmental practices to assess and distinguish the unemployed able-bodied poor from the disabled were often refined. Even as far back as 1697, for instance, the Badging Act had required everyone who relied on parish relief to wear a badge that declared their initials and pauper status. In turn, subsequent laws further constructed disability as a categorisation for state intervention, as we will return to in the following chapter.

In this context, Descartes' proposal, while initially considered heretical, would come to be so widely adopted not just because it was useful for medicine. It was also enormously useful for capital, since by the nineteenth century, the industrialists, plantation owners, and other capitalists had come to see their workers as individual machines who could be working or broken. And by this time, it was the needs of the capitalists more primarily than the scriptures of the church that determined what was acceptable.

So it came to be, as Karl Marx was perhaps the first to observe in 1867, that capitalism brought not just new machines, but also an 'artificially produced' transformation of 'human beings into mere machines for the production of surplus-value'.[22] And as we shall see in the next chapter, it was here – in these new standards of mechanistic functioning – that the emerging statistical concept of 'normality' would come to replace the traditional concept of equilibrium when it came to understanding health.

2

The invention of normality

Alongside the shift from humoral to mechanistic conceptions of bodily functioning came another shift, no less important, from viewing health as *harmony* to viewing health as *normality*. It is to this shift, beginning with the story of a pioneering Belgian statistician called Adolphe Quetelet, that we now turn. What Quetelet did was propose the first science of human normality, which laid the grounds for later work in medicine, criminology, psychology, and eugenics. This made him one of the leading early social scientists, whose influence still impacts our lives today. Yet as we shall see, this was not simply a matter of scientific discovery. As with the rise of the machine metaphor, it would be a reflection of the economic and ideological shifts of the age. In part, this was the same industrialisation that led to the reinterpretation of humans as machines. But this time it was also the bourgeois revolutions in France and Belgium.

To understand Quetelet's work, we need to first turn back to the origins of statistics that grounded his thinking. Interestingly, basic conceptions of the 'average' in the modern sense, associated with a summary of data, did not emerge among the medics. In fact, statistical analysis had first been developed by astronomers in the sixteenth century to predict the course of planets that could not always be observed. This then progressed in bits and pieces over the following centuries until 1801. It was in this year that the German mathematician Carl Friedrich Gauss was able to develop a formula on which he based a bell curve shaped graph, predicting the movement of a star named Ceres. This became known as the 'error curve', where errors were understood as deviations from the norm. It was this that opened the way for early statistical analyses of normality to be used in other fields for summarising data. It was also this that allowed the normal to be associated with correctness, and abnormality with error.

In medicine, such concepts were first applied following the French Revolution, which lasted from 1789 to 1799. The revolution had attempted to free humans from religious dogma, traditional customs, and the feudal system. The new form of state that emerged required the quantification and counting of everything in standardised ways free from the taint of supernatural beliefs or provincial customs. This led to new statistical and quantitative approaches to just about everything, including the development of the metric system, the standardisation of weights, map-making surveys, and much more. These would purport to be universal and objective, allowing new ways of organising and improving society.

At the same time, the revolution also brought a great many injuries, deaths, and executions, which meant that physicians in Paris were free to begin documenting and experimentally applying new statistical ideas to their abundant supply of patients, bodies, and records. As the historians Cryle and Stephens have established, the term 'normal state' thus first appeared in French literature on comparative anatomy in around 1820 before being used in medical texts in the 1830s, although at this time it was only used in passing and had neither a clear definition nor an obvious scientific use.[1]

Within this context, the most important early theoretical intervention came from Quetelet. Born in Ghent – then part of the French Republic – in 1796, Quetelet had studied mathematics and astronomy, receiving a doctorate from the University of Ghent in 1819. He soon became known as a talented lecturer and keen musician, who would entertain guests with recitals during dinner parties. In the 1820s Quetelet then proposed the development of a new observatory. This gained support from the government, so he travelled to France and England to learn more about the latest instruments and methods in astronomy. Guided by his new knowledge, he then returned and began constructing a new observatory of his own.

Quetelet's running of the observatory was interrupted, however, by the revolution of 1830 that restored independence to Belgium. Following the disruption of the revolution – during which his obser-

35

vatory was occupied and used as an armoury – he became more interested in using statistics to understand and predict the social world instead of the physical world. While he published some brief articles earlier, it was his ground-breaking 1835 book *The Average Man* (*l'homme moyen*) that became an international hit and earned him his place in the history of statistics, medicine, and social science.

What Quetelet proposed was a radical new science of human normality. His suggestion, in his own words, was that:

the weight and stature of a man may be measured directly, and we may afterwards compare them with the weight and stature of another man. In comparing the different men of a nation in this manner, we arrive at average values, which are the weight and stature proper to be assigned to the average man.[2]

By studying records of Scottish soldiers, he was able to make averages of height, weight, and so forth to understand and predict the nature of the typical Scotsman. Based on this, Quetelet argued that the concept of the average man would be helpful for understanding the 'normal state' of health. This is perhaps best exemplified by Quetelet's development of, among much else, the very Body Mass Index, or BMI, formula that is still used today to measure whether people are under, or over, their ideal weight. This also allowed notions such as the average heart rate, or normal lung capacity, to be developed over the following century.[3] This allowed human mechanistic functioning to not just be understood as working or broken, but to be assessed and ranked in ever-more fine-grained ways in relation to whatever was considered normal.

Yet like the shift to the machine metaphor, this too was not simply a matter of scientific progress. To understand it fully, we must recognise how it mirrored shifts in social and material relations. It was not just that this helped ground a mechanistic science of the body, allowing for recognition of different levels of functioning. Quetelet also posited the average man as the ideal person of post-revolution France in a way that helped create a new ideal: 'If the average man were completely determined', he wrote, we might 'consider him as the type of perfection; and everything differing from his proportions or condition, would constitute', he went on, 'a monstrosity'.[4] In making this leap, Quetelet helped solidify the association of the average man not just with health but also with moral goodness and perfection. The error curve developed to predict the course of stars now applied to human normativity, and to be abnormal was to be a mistake of nature.

To understand this, it is important to bear in mind, as Allan Horwitz has noted, that, in line with the ideals of the French Revolution, Quetelet's 'view was radically democratic because each individual, from the most noble to the most downtrodden, had equivalent weight to every other one' for the first time.[5] Yet simultaneously, as Lennard Davis writes,

> In formulating the idea of *l'homme moyen*, Quetelet is also providing a justification for *les classes moyens*. With bourgeois hegemony comes scientific justification for moderation and middle-class ideology. The average man, the body of the man in the middle, becomes the exemplar of the middle way of life. [This ideology thus] saw the bourgeoisie as rationally placed in the mean position in the great order of things.[6]

Simultaneously, Quetelet's 'average man' was also determined specifically in relation to the nation-state. The perfect man in France would be different to the perfect man from Germany, who would again be different to the perfect average in Russia. In each of these nations, those who sat further from the average man of the specific nation – consider, say, a Black man in a white majority nation – would be considered comparatively monstrous. Hence the new average man concept helped provide a way of normalising racial nationalism alongside bourgeois hegemony.

Overall, then, the notion of the average man did not just help medicine advance. It also helped naturalise the new ideology and hierarchies that emerged as the last remnants of feudalism gave way to the dominance of capitalism in France and beyond. In European nations – where nationalism was rising as empires vied for control of colonies around the world – the average man would be a white, middle-class man of typical ability. And he, rather than, say, the king or high priest, now exemplified all that was good and proper, while those who deviated from normality were monstrous and in need of fixing.

THE MEAN UNDERSTANDING

We also see similar material forces at play in the related idea of the 'mean understanding'. In earlier times, philosophers such as Aristotle, working in Athens, and Abu Bakr al-Razi, working in Baghdad, had written extensively on the intellect.[7] But the British notion of the 'mean understanding' was developed for a practical purpose, initially being constructed around the notion of idiocy as capitalism dawned in England. Prior to the Enlightenment, idiocy had mainly been viewed through a religious lens. Those called idiots were sometimes seen as monstrous, but were equally often seen as vulnerable members of the community deserving of support. Indeed, some even led relatively privileged lives in court. This was because they were widely taken to have access to divine wisdom, and it was thought by some that keeping a fool would absolve one's sins.[8] More generally, in medieval and feudal societies, as the historian Roddy Sloarch details, the

lives of people with impairments were determined by the general conditions of exploitation and oppression that obtained in these (often brutal societies). But there is no evidence of any specific, systemic discrimination levelled at them.[9]

However, in seventeenth-century England, which was then beginning to develop into a global superpower, the concept of the 'mean understanding' emerged. And along with this we do precisely see new forms of discrimination.

Interestingly, this was initially in the specific context of legal disputes relating to the inheritance of private property. The concept of the mean understanding was essentially developed to exclude people with cognitive disabilities from inheriting property, and to allow distant family members with 'normal' levels of understanding to be able to (usually unfairly) extract that property. We can see, for instance, how as far back as 1700 the English Lawyer John Brydall's book *Non Compos Mentis: Or, The Law Relating to Natural Fools,* was full of claims such as the following:

If a Man be of a mean understanding (neither of the wisest sort, nor of the foolish'st) but, indifferent as it were, betwixt a Wise man and a Fool, yea though he rather incline to the foolish sort, so that for his dull capacity he might worthily be termed Grossum Caput, a dull Pate, Dunce, such a one is not prohibited to make a Testament.[10]

The proposal that those lower on this ranking should be prohibited from making a testament essentially means that their testimony, and, by implication, their interests, should have no legal standing in property disputes. At the same time, the new concept of 'natural fools' allowed such mistreatments to be seen as part of the natural order. Hence, the concept of the 'mean understanding' initially took hold because it allowed cognitively enabled people to make sure they had a monopoly on property and the means of production – and to begin to frame this as part of a natural hierarchy.[11]

However, early capitalist conceptions of the 'mean understanding' were not based on a statistical analysis, since prior to Quetelet, there were neither methods nor data to derive the mean. Soundness of mind was only very loosely determined by legal professionals who would ask questions about general knowledge or mathematics to determine legal competence. It was only following Quetelet's influence, and in line with the start of the Industrial Revolution in England, that various attempts to apply statistical methods to the brain and mind emerged, usually in order to reify emerging hierarchical distinctions in ability, social class, gender, and race.[12]

Among the most significant early examples of this is phrenology, developed by the physician Franz Gall in 1796. Back when he was a student, Gall had noticed that his classmates with larger eyes and foreheads seemed better at memorising long passages of text. He soon began to wonder whether these surface differences indicated underlying differences in brain structure and functioning. In time he came to think that mental functioning mapped onto specific brain regions which could be read through the shape of the skull. Phrenology, purported to be a new science, thus sought to link head shape with mental faculties to determine mental ability, character, and even propensity for criminality.

While phrenology would later come to be seen as a pseudo-science, in industrial Britain many of its proponents believed that they could use the emerging notion of normality to ground its scientific aspirations. In 1845, for instance, James Straton, a Scottish phrenologist, explained in his book *Contributions to the Mathematics of Phrenology* that his aim was to develop 'a scale, indicating the average size, the average range, and the extreme ranges of size which have been found among the various races of men'.[13] For Straton, skulls and brains that were too big or small would be contrasted with what he called the 'healthy normal structure, and competent mental capacity to fulfil the imperative duties of life'.[14]

Despite not being properly scientific, phrenology was important because it was so influential in contributing to an emerging shift in cultural understandings relating to race, cognition, and social class. By this time, it is important to remember, European empires built on genocide and colonialism encompassed most of the globe. White Europeans had come to see themselves as superior to other races, upon whose enslaved labour their power depended. The bodies of Africans and indigenous men and especially women were seen in England as monstrous and deformed, while mentally they were seen as somewhere between humans and beasts.[15] The class system was also deeply entrenched, and the working classes were often seen by members of the ruling classes as having an inherently lower ability to reason.

Within this context, as Sysling details, phrenology not only 'introduced the "average" to the masses, no matter how little factual basis it had. It provided, both in the United States and in the United Kingdom, a new way for white middle-class men and women to position themselves in an imagined statistical collective'.[16] Phrenology was supported by figures ranging from the philosopher Herbert Spencer to the eminent biologist Alfred Wallace. Indeed, even Queen Victoria herself consulted a famous phrenologist, who she asked to read the heads of her children. Given its widespread support, it helped bring a mass shift in collective understanding of both ourselves and each other, and where each of us sat in a natural hierarchy of minds.

Through such cultural practices the concept of the normal mind and brain merged with capitalist and colonial ideology, promising to provide a purportedly objective grounding that could naturalise the cognitive, economic and racial hierarchies that had already begun to emerge in the centuries prior. In this process, ancient conceptions of wisdom or the intellect began to be replaced by a new way of understanding, grounded in statistics. The ideal spread, and middle-class, cognitively abled white people increasingly came to see themselves as naturally closer to an idealised 'normal', even super-normal, way of being and thinking when compared to disabled, working-class, and Black and Brown colonised subjects. To have any kind of subnormal cognition was increasingly feared and stigmatised, especially among the upper classes in Europe as well as among white settlers around the globe.

THE GREAT CONFINEMENT

All the factors detailed here and in the previous chapter did not bring a shift in understanding alone. Beyond the use of legal conceptions of the mean understanding to appropriate property from people with cognitive disabilities, a related shift that accompanied the rise of capitalism was the rise of a range of interrelated carceral systems. For those called the mad – which included the cognitively disabled – this led to what Michel Foucault, in his classic 1961 book *Madness and Civilisation*,[17] called the 'great confinement'. As Foucault details, in the renaissance, mad people were often depicted as having divine wisdom and were often included in the community. As with the disabled, while life was hard for them as for everyone else, they were not systematically discriminated against specifically by virtue of their madness.

By contrast, as was noted above, late feudalism and then capitalism brought a boom in population density and a great increase in poverty. This generated worries about population control and productivity. In this context, alongside begging, sex work, petty crime, and other things deemed outrageous to bourgeois morality, madness came to be seen as a problem to be solved by locking people up. What each of these groups were taken to share with the others was idleness, which was at odds with the capitalist demand for productivity. The mad in particular were also seen as an affront to the Enlightenment ideal of rationality, and thus as a threat to civilisation itself.

While the extent of the confinement emphasised by Foucault remains controversial among historians,[18] it is indisputable that asylums emerged in this period, and that the mad – including people with cognitive disability – were often chained up, isolated, and subject to physical punishments. It is also clear that by the nineteenth century, there was an ever-increasing segregation of the able poor into workhouses, the criminalised into prisons, and the mad into asylums. New legislation, most notably the New Poor Law of 1834, intended to reduce the cost of poor relief, made it mandatory for parishes to construct workhouses if they did not have one already. Thus, as capitalism further developed and the population grew, its norms hardened, with the abnormal becoming ever-more salient as more of the population fell beyond its new standards of functioning. It was this that necessitated the mass development of these new carceral systems, which, all in their own ways, imprisoned those deemed abnormal.

As larger state institutions were built across Europe, the confinement and management of the mad spread to the colonies of the European empires, fusing with racist ideology to delineate new discourses. Writing from Britain, for instance, the influential psychiatrist Henry Maudsley – whom the Maudsley Hospital in South London was later named after – wrote of the 'comparative inferiority' of the brains of indigenous 'bushwomen',[19] when compared to white Europeans. Building on this, in sub-Saharan Africa British psychiatrists soon began pontificating on the extent to which 'normal' Africans had similarities to insane Europeans, on the grounds that purported 'superstition, primitive beliefs' and 'incapacity for abstract thought' manifested in both populations.[20]

Within this context, it is around the mid-nineteenth century that we finally see the birth of psychiatry as a branch of medicine. This accompanied a more general shift in the purported function of asylums. When the asylums had first emerged, they were made primarily to provide a way to keep the mad away from the rest of society. But by around 1850 – just as Quetelet's notion of the normal state was becoming increasingly influential in a range of scientific pursuits – the emphasis was moved to viewing inmates not as threats to be contained, but as patients to be treated, or returned to normality.

This came partly from the influence of earlier liberal reformers. The most notable was the influential French physician Phillipe Pinel, who sought to turn the asylums into places of what he called 'moral therapy' rather than imprisonment and torture. More broadly, as Andrew Scull has detailed, it was partly the role of 'mad doctors' in the asylums that allowed a shift from 'the vague cultural view of madness' into the idea that it was an identifiable and treatable condition.[21] And yet equally important, Scull goes on, was that industrial capitalism had led the labour pool to be increasingly seen as:

> manipulable human material whose yield could be steadily enlarged through careful management and through improvements in use and organization, rationally designed to transform its value as an economic resource.[22]

The rise of capitalism – through its colonial roots and then imperial stages – thus finally brought the modern notion that the mad need to be treated, to ease their suffering and return the idle to the workforce. It was in this new context of viewing the population as a malleable economic resource that we see the emergence of new professional roles that paved the way for early pre-paradigmatic psychiatry and related disciplines such as psychology and psycho-metrics to emerge. And the new mechanistic understanding of the body and mind, coupled with new conceptions of normality, brought a new way of grounding these projects. As we will see in the next chapter, this would then be combined with the emerging statistical notions of normal functioning to ground not just the rise of eugenics but also the psychiatric paradigm that still exists today – the pathology paradigm.

NORMALITY AND CAPITALISM

At this point I want to pause to summarise what we have covered so far. Traditionally – across the globe – both mental and bodily health were typically conceptualised as a matter of balance or equilibrium. This was either within the body or between body and environment. But the capitalist mode of production and the Industrial Revolution began to bring a new conception of health and ability. The body and mind were increasingly seen as machines, and the new concept of normality began to be used to determine whether these machines were working or broken. And far from being a merely technical medical concept, the idea of normality began to bring a profound shift in how different individuals and classes of people came to see themselves. It also came with new forms of administration of populations. This provided white, cognitively abled, middle-class people to justify the various hierarchies that had emerged given the rise of capitalism as well as colonialism and imperialism. It also allowed cognitively abled people to begin establishing a monopoly on property and the means of production. As such, the normality concept mirrored contingent social hierarchies while at the same time framing these hierarchies as natural.

Here, then, we see the beginning of what I call the Empire of Normality. This new apparatus, made up of a complex nexus of different carceral systems, legal precedents, institutions, concepts, and practices, led to populations beginning to be systematically ranked in terms of mental and neurological ability, while positing this as part of a timeless natural order. This was not an accident, but was rather built into the logics of capitalism from the beginning. And it was in this context, as we will come to next, that a British polymath named Francis Galton developed the pathology paradigm – the precise paradigm the neurodiversity movement would later arise to name and resist.

3

Galton's paradigm

Francis Galton was born in Birmingham in 1822 to a family of bankers and gun-manufacturers. The grandson of Erasmus Darwin and half-cousin of Charles Darwin, Galton himself was a rather strange child prodigy, learning to read by the age of two and quickly excelling in his education from that time. He went on to study medicine at King's College London and mathematics at Cambridge, just around the time that Quetelet's pathbreaking work was being widely discussed in both fields. After his father died, the young Galton's vast inheritance allowed him to travel, invent, write, and, in time, become among the most influential scientists of his generation.

To understand Galton's work, it is important to note that he soon became obsessed with genius – a term he identified with – as well as with ranking humans in every way imaginable. This dated at least back to when, as a young man, Galton was incredibly impressed by a phrenologist he visited. While we do not know precisely what he was told, it is safe to assume that, as a Victorian gentleman, he would have been considered close to the top of their imagined statistical order. In turn, Galton became equally obsessed with heredity, hypothesising while studying at Cambridge that the fact Cambridge was full of middle-class white men might indicate that this demographic was constitutionally superior to everyone else. In this, he saw the hierarchies of the British Empire not as contingent and based on specific historical factors, but rather as an expression of natural superiority that could be scientifically verified.

It was in pursuing these obsessions that Galton would go on to become an influential statistician and to help found a variety of fields, including psychometrics, behavioural genetics, and the pseudo-science eugenics (the last of these being a term he coined). It is curious that, despite his influence being acknowl-edged elsewhere, Galton is barely mentioned in general histories of psychiatry, whether those written by mainstream psychiatrists or anti-psychiatry critics. Yet it is my contention that he was the founder of the pathology paradigm, in the sense that he provided both its metaphysical basis and developed many of the experimen-tal methods that provided blueprints for later researchers. And it was this – Galton's paradigm – that would then be taken up by Emil Kraepelin, often described as the 'father' of modern psychiatry, and other influential clinicians and researchers across the psycholog-ical sciences. This would form the basis of the approach that has remained dominant to this very day, and which functions to natu-ralise and scientifically legitimise the neuronormative domination of capitalism as it continues to develop.

EVOLUTIONARY RANKING

For our purposes, a key part of Galton's contribution was to fuse his half-cousin's ideas about natural selection, published in *On the Origin of Species* in 1859,[1] with Quetelet's statistical analysis of pop-ulations, this time, in his own words, applying the 'same law to mental faculties'.[2] By bringing these together Galton began a more formal and intentional project of scientific cultural normalisation that came to impact every corner of modern society.

Looking back, it is hard to understate the significance of Darwin's impact on how humans came to understand ourselves. People had known for millennia that traits seemed to be inherited to some extent, and Darwin's contemporaries had proposed various theories to help explain this. Yet Darwin's theory of evolution, which sug-gested that natural selection occurred through a combination of random mutations and fittingness to environment, was the first to have strong evidence and explanatory force. Darwin's own painstak-ingly detailed observations and explanations forced a fundamental reconsidering of the human as not just a machine, but one who shared common ancestors with other primates. As such – and in comparison to Descartes' attempt to preserve the sanctity of the soul – the Darwinian mind was no less a product of evolutionary design, and hence nature, than the rest of the body. Darwin essentially thus provided the human and biological sciences with new levels of respectability while opening up a host of new possible developments.

In this context, Galton saw a viable ground to move beyond Quetelet's reliance on pre-scientific notions of human 'perfection' and 'monstrosity'. What Galton took from Darwin, more specifically, was the notion that variation is ubiquitous, and in turn that different organisms will have different fitness levels given their different natural abilities. Underlying this too was the Darwinian theory of evolution, which could explain variation among different human individuals and races. For Galton, this meant that each individual could be more or less fit when compared to others, and this could be framed as a matter of evolutionary functioning or adaptiveness.

While he had published some briefer articles earlier, his 1869 book *Hereditary Genius* is notable for combining Darwin's theory with Quetelet's statistical methods to analyse intelligence over different generations. Thus, Galton's proposal, in his own words, was to:

> range men according to their natural abilities, putting them into classes separated by equal degrees of merit [...] The method I shall employ for discovering this is an application of the very curious theoretical law of 'deviation from the average'.[3]

Galton's initial attempt was based on comparing heredity across a range of records of individuals, family trees, and races and judging them in terms of 'eminence'. This essentially led him to rank white, upper-class Europeans, and the Ancient Greeks, at the top and Black Africans and indigenous Australians at the bottom. Women – who, Galton thought, were unlikely to be geniuses – did not even appear in his rankings. Hence his book essentially functioned to naturalise the racialised, abled, economic, and gendered hierarchies of the British Empire.

Hereditary Genius was initially met with mixed reviews. On the one hand, Galton's work was supported by Darwin, who described

48

it as 'interesting and original'[4] and Alfred Wallace who described it as 'ingenious'.[5] Yet many others recognised that Galton's analysis relied on a great many biased assumptions regarding the extent of heredity, the validity of judgements of 'eminence', and influence of social class. One reviewer, for instance, noted that Galton ascribed eminence to 'men of very average ability, helped forward by incidental advantages' while overlooking circumstances and early education.[6]

Such critiques, however, did not deter Galton. His inherited wealth allowed him to continue his work, and in the following decades he went on to develop a variety of early methods for psychometric and biometric testing. These ranged from the first intelligence tests to the first biometric technology. It was these that he used in his psychological laboratory in London – the first of its kind – where he could study and record individual abilities of huge numbers of people to generate statistical norms. From this laboratory Galton pioneered new methods including psychological questionnaires alongside developing a range of devices for testing abilities such as cognitive reaction times. This led to a new notion of individual ability that was cut off from environment and reified as having its own set value. As Danziger writes

What Galton's testing situation produced was essentially a set of individual *performances* that could be compared with each other [that] defined characteristics of independent, socially isolated individuals and these characteristics were designated as 'abilities'. An ability was what a person could do on his own, and the object of interest was either the individual defined as an assembly of such abilities or the distribution of performance abilities in a population.[7]

Like the phrenologists who influenced him, this thus allowed Galton to locate specific individual abilities that he would rank through statistical analysis. Moreover, he sought to map this onto inherited biological traits. His method of twin studies was proposed to distinguish between 'nature and nurture' – another enduring phrase

Galton coined – that could be used to help see to what extent ability, character, or disposition was heritable.[8] This, along with seminal work on the regression of the height of sweet peas over different generations,[9] allowed Galton to found the field of behavioural genetics and to suggest that a species could 'regress' if not properly controlled.

It is important to recognise that Galton did not design these methods for purely scientific purposes. He used them to obsessively rank just about any aspect of human life. Among other things, for instance, he was the first man to statistically rank women from different areas in terms of attractiveness. Not only was this determined by his own judgements, it was also done in secret, with a clicker he used in his pocket whenever he saw a woman out in public. This began a misogynistic tradition of numerically ranking women that continues to this day. Facebook, for instance, was first made as a site for ranking the attractiveness of female college students, before it grew into the social media giant it is today.

It was also Galton that proved identity could be detected through fingerprinting technology, thus paving the way for scientific control of the criminalised. In this, he helped formalise a technique that would allow the prison industrial complex to grow rapidly. In his laboratory, he recorded both the mental abilities and biometric markers of thousands of Londoners, generating aggregates and analysing individuals in relation to statistical norms to judge their worth. It was his work on mental ability that paved the way for subsequent intelligence tests developed by Alfred Binet and Théodore Simon – and grounded the psychometric and biometric research methods used in the following century.

Just as importantly, with Galton we see not just the development of new methods but also an ideological shift. Despite Quetelet's influence, Galton eventually came to suggest that the average was, while better than sub-normality, still something to be *overcome* rather than being the ideal state as Quetelet had envisioned. Essentially Galton was more interested in variation and rank, with the average sitting in the middle of his ranking rather than being seen as a form of perfection in itself. This was primarily based on his

interest in genius and idiocy, but also on his fears of racial degener-
ation, and the idea, in his own words, that those who 'deviate widely
from the mean' risk the race's reversion to 'that mediocrity, whence
the majority of their ancestors originally sprang'.[10]

While it is apparent, in retrospect, that Galton's misogyny, racism,
and class ideology drove much of his thinking, it is notable that
he was quite explicit in the significance of productivity in his later
ranking systems. 'Energy', he wrote in 1883, 'is the capacity for
labour' and is 'consistent with all the robust virtues, and makes a
large practice of them possible'. In turn, he went on, energy 'is the
measure of fulness of life; the more energy the more abundance of it;
no energy at all is death; idiots are feeble and listless'. And of course,
he also associated higher productivity with what he took to be racial
superiority, positing that energy is 'an attribute of the higher races,
being favoured beyond all other qualities by natural selection'.[11]
Hence his later work moved away from the more unambiguously
value-laden notion of 'eminence' and instead sought to associate
fitness with productivity in order to ground it in, so he thought, a
more objective Darwinian analysis.

Yet as Donald Mackenzie later put it, in Galton and his followers
we see 'the practice and experience of the intellectual aristocracy
read onto nature'.[12] Mackenzie's work links this precisely to the class
structures in Britain at the time. In his own words:

The core of this view was the idea that social position was (or
at least should be) the consequence of individual mental ability.
There was a natural hierarchy of talent which could be translated into a social hierarchy of occupations. At the top were the
professions, with leading businessmen sometimes admitted into
the elite: they represented the pick of the nation's brains. Below
them were useful but increasingly dull-brained groups: small
businessmen, clerks, shop-keepers, foremen, skilled workers.
These were socially valuable, if not as valuable as the professional.
Finally, there came strata who were typically stupid or worse: the
unskilled, the unemployed and the outcast.[13]

In this, according to Mackenzie, the statistical and methodological innovations developed by Galton were not simply objective discoveries. Rather, while they did have scientific utility, they were simultaneously innovations that reflected and in turn helped naturalise the ideology of the time. In turn, their uses in scientific research would help to naturalise the cognitive, economic, gendered, and racial hierarchies of capitalist and imperialist Britain.

Ultimately, what all this would lead toward would be Galton's proposal of the new science of 'eugenics' in the 1880s. Initially, it was Galton's concern with surpassing the average that inspired the key theoretical change underlying what he referred to as the 'method of statistics by intercomparison'.[14] This consisted largely in substituting Quetelet's mean for the median. The disability historian Lennard Davis has emphasised how it was this shift in statistical method that was used to justify Galton's attempts to rank individuals and populations from the most to least fit. For while 'high intelligence in a' Quetelian 'normal distribution would simply be an extreme' and thus undesirable, under a Galtonian 'system it would become the highest ranked trait'.[15] As Galton wrote in 1883, the 'median value may be accepted as the average' due to representing not the ideal, but rather the 'multitude of mediocre values' between the highest and the lowest abilities.[16]

It was this shift that allowed Galton to present his newly coined concept of eugenics. He defined eugenics as: 'the science of improving stock [...] to give to the more suitable races or strains of blood a better chance of prevailing'.[17] Based on his new methods for ranking individuals and groups, Galton argued that the role of governments should be to improve the average range of successive generations. And thus it was precisely with Galton's work, as Stephens and Cryle have stressed, that 'the idea of the application of normal as a cultural practice' finally emerged.[18] In other words, Galton formalised, and provided a veneer of scientific legitimacy to, the informal normalising practices we covered in the previous chapter. It was this that would legitimise a mass expansion of these practices over the following decades – and, as we shall come back to, would in time be used to justify some of the worst atrocities ever committed.

KRAEPELIN'S GALTONIANISATION OF PSYCHIATRY

We have just considered how Galton began to develop the idea of the normal mind in such a way that allowed him to rank the mental functioning of individuals and groups from the lowest to highest. This was taken up in a range of sciences. The influence of Galton on psychological and psychometric research has been well established elsewhere. The most notable work on this is Kurt Danziger's book *Constructing the Subject: Historical Origins of Psychological Research*, which establishes how Galton's theories and methods formed the basis for much research since this time. As was noted above, Galton is also widely acknowledged as having provided much of the basis for behavioural genetics. By contrast, his influence has been curiously overlooked in psychiatry, and Galton is barely mentioned in general histories of the discipline.

Yet Galton's influence on psychiatry was in fact highly significant. While he inspired a number of doctors, the most notable to expand Galton's paradigm was the most prominent of all nineteenth-century German psychiatrists, Emil Kraepelin. Today, Kraepelin is widely credited with developing the biocentric, classificatory approach adopted both in the German psychiatry that dominated during his time before being reborn in the DSM from 1980 onward. His legacy is typically associated with his quest to turn psychiatry into a firmly scientific discipline, continuous with general medicine. In large part, he is taken to have done this through adopting a naturalistic and experimental approach, alongside attention to classifications he sought to map on to biological aetiology. Viewed in the context covered here, however, it would be more accurate to say that Kraepelin – who, in his autobiography, recalled Galton as a 'fine old gentleman, who stimulated the field of psychology'[19] – essentially expanded the scope of Galton's paradigm.

Kraepelin himself was born in 1856 in a small town in the north of Germany called Neustrelitz. When Kraepelin began studying psychology and medicine at the University of Leipzig, both psychology and psychiatry had only just begun to emerge in response to the broader economic and historical shifts detailed in the previous chapters. They were not yet proper sciences with anything like a coherent unifying paradigm. In fact, Kraepelin himself had initially been more inspired by his teacher Wilhelm Wundt, whose pioneering experimental psychology focused on individual introspection and not collective aggregates. Yet by the early twentieth century, the Wundtian method had deteriorated while the Galtonian approach was, as Danziger writes, 'extending its appeal with every passing year' as 'it proved itself capable of generating exciting methodological innovations that promised to extend the scope of scientific psychology far beyond what had hitherto been thought possible'.[20] And it was in this approach, which was then fast becoming accepted as the correct basis for psychological, psychometric, and biometric research, that Kraepelin envisioned the grounds for a new, scientific psychiatry.

While much of Kraepelin's work focused on clinical understanding, we see the Galtonian influence when we consider his more theoretical work. This was stated most clearly in Kraepelin's 1919 essay 'Ends and Means of Psychiatric Research', where he proposed an unmistakably Galtonian vision for the future of what he termed 'mass psychiatry'. In his own words:

> By [...] determining the range of normal variation, we shall obtain a standard for measuring morbid deviations – a standard that will be of value, not merely for pure science, but for many practical purposes, as for estimating school capacity, military fitness, business talent, and responsibility [...] Thus we may gradually learn, not only to characterise numerically the various grades amid kinds of intellectual defect, but to obtain more exact expressions for insufficiencies and aberrances in other mental spheres. Only thus can the important forms of psychopathy that fade into one another be more clearly outlined.[21]

In other words, what Kraepelin envisioned was expanding the approach Galton had developed to study intelligence. It would now encompass every other aspect of the mind, including as a basis for psychiatry but also for a variety of roles in relation to the shifting needs of capital in education, the workplace, and so forth. The hope was that expanding this method would allow a greater and more specific understanding of a wide range of dysfunctions that could then be treated and controlled.

In turn, for Kraepelin, the ends of psychiatry, and its use of these methods, likewise echoed the Galtonian hope for bio-cultural normalisation and improvement. As Kraepelin put it:

The psychiatric importance of such investigation on the large scale cannot be over-estimated. A mass psychiatry, having at its disposal statistics in their widest scope, must provide the foundations for a science of public mental health – a preventive psychological medicine for combating all those mischiefs that we group under the head of mental degeneracy.[22]

Part of the worry here, Kraepelin went on, was that 'an ever-widening stream of inferior stock [is mixing] itself with our offspring, [contributing] to the deterioration of the race'.[23] Thus, for Kraepelin as for Galton, the concept of the normal mind was utilised precisely because it grounded the broader political project of biological and cultural control.

It was through this underlying framework that Kraepelin began the still ongoing project of dividing up mental disorders into different kinds and levels of subnormal functioning, with a focus on heredity, severity, development, and outcome throughout the lifespan. And in turn this approach was adopted in German psychiatry – which was very much a world leader in the psychiatry of the time – thus allowing a growing number of new classifications to be specified, studied, and controlled.

Indeed, eugenic thinking became so popular among psychiatrists that it was even included in influential textbooks of the time. Most notable here was the psychiatrist Eugene Bleuler, known for coining the terms 'schizophrenia' and 'autism'. In his 1924 Textbook of Psychiatry, Bleuler openly stated his view that the 'more severely burdened should not propagate themselves' in case the race would 'rapidly deteriorate'.[24] Thus Kraepelin and his contemporaries expanded the Galtonian paradigm to form the basis for modern psychiatry, while the same metaphysics came to underpin the emerging fields of clinical, abnormal, and developmental psychology.

4

The eugenics movement

We first see the political and cultural effects of Galton's eugenic ideology in Britain. Inspired by Galton, the Eugenic Education Society was founded in 1906 (renamed as the Eugenics Society in 1924 and then as the Galton Institute in 1989).[1] In the early days the society included prominent members such as the economist John Maynard Keynes, the biologist Julian Huxley, and Galton himself. Among many other proposals, the society endorsed involuntary euthanasia of the 'feeble-minded' alongside funds for the wealthy to reproduce in higher numbers. While the British government rejected the Eugenic Education Society's proposals for compulsory sterilisation of the feeble-minded, it did vote in the 1913 Mental Deficiency Act to begin mass segregation based on proximity to cognitive normality. Winston Churchill himself stated in the Act's support that the 'unnatural and increasingly rapid growth of the feeble-minded classes, coupled with a steady restriction among the thrifty, energetic and superior stocks constitutes a race danger'.[2]

In the United States, the Americanism 'normalcy' had been introduced to the broader public following the First World War, when 'return to normalcy' was used as Warren Harding's 1920 presidential election campaign slogan (despite 'normalcy' not yet appearing in dictionaries). This period was accompanied – building on the cultural foundations laid by phrenology – by the further rise of Galtonian aspirations among members of the public. This can be seen in the 'better baby' or 'fitter family' contests that spread across the United States between the 1910s and 1930s. As Stern explains

the contests began at the Iowa State Fair in 1911 when clubwoman Mary T. Watts asked, 'You are raising better cattle, better horses,

57

and better hogs, why don't you raise better babies?' To judge infants like livestock, Watts and another rural reformer, Margaret Clark, devised scorecards that tallied level of physical health, anthropometric traits, and mental development.[3]

As such contests spread, eugenics classes were also increasingly taught in many US universities, and eugenic policies were adopted in a variety of states. Women with intellectual disabilities – especially Black women – were forcibly sterilised, and people with cognitive disabilities were prevented from emigrating. Black disabled women in particular were seen not just as economic burdens but also threats to the purity of the white race.[4]

It is important to note here that the ideology of normality was not only embraced on the right. Indeed, even Karl Marx's concept of the 'average worker' was directly influenced by Quetelet.[5] While Marx died in 1883 and would have never heard of eugenics, many on the left came to embrace Galton's ideals. For instance, Sidney Webb, the co-founder of the London School of Economics, early member of the Fabian Society, and an influential socialist, lamented in 1896 about the 'wrong production, both of commodities and of human beings; the preparation of senseless luxuries whilst there is need for more bread, and the breeding of degenerate hordes of a demoralized "residuum" unfit for social life'.[6] The socialist and philosopher Bertrand Russell made similarly eugenicist proposals, writing in 1927 that by 'sterilizing the feeble-minded of two generations, feeble-mindedness and idiocy could be almost stamped out'.[7] Similarly, women's rights campaigners such as Marie Stopes advocated compulsory sterilisation and suggested that birth control could improve British stock.[8] In turn – as I shall return to later – eugenic ideas were also adopted in the Soviet Union, with the Russian Eugenics Society being founded in 1920 and Marxists such as Alexander Serebrovsky arguing for mass eugenics programmes.[9]

Eugenicists drawing on the Galtonian research paradigm also had considerable influence over policy. For instance, following educational segregation in Britain, the post-war separation of children into three types of school – technical (for those good at practical trades), grammar (for those considered academic) and secondary modern (for everyone else) – was in significant part based on reasoning from Cyril Burt. Burt, who was a psychology professor and at one point a president of the British Psychological Society, was also a eugenicist who suggested that intelligence was innate and heritable. He claimed that children could be divided into three key kinds of intelligence, based on which British children of 'normal' ability were split into different kinds of schools in a system that still persists today – despite it later being found that Burt had fabricated the data from his twin studies.

Being endorsed across the political spectrum in the imperial core, eugenic ideology and policy were also exported to colonies. The historian Chloe Campbell has detailed how the British eugenics movement in particular became the 'intellectual mother ship'[10] for the spread of eugenic ideology and policy to colonies globally. This was often led by doctors and colonial officials who founded different eugenics organisations across the world. The specifics of their policies, however, depended on how local populations were racially positioned. For instance, the Kenyan Society for the Study of Race Improvement was founded in 1933. But in contrast to British eugenics – and despite the name of the society – the aim was to limit the population rather than to improve it. For since the Kenyan population was predominantly Black it was assumed by white officials that mental deficiency affected the entire population rather than only the working class and disabled.

NAZI EUGENICS

Galton, after dedicating the last few decades of his life to eugenics, died in 1911. By this time, he had published over 340 books or articles and was a world-famous polymath. His writings on eugenics had inspired a global movement made up of the leading politicians, scientists, and philosophers of the generation. Still, he was worried that his ideas hadn't yet reached a wide enough audience. In his final years he had thus been working on a novel titled *Kantsaywhere*, which was about a utopian society of the same name. This society was ruled through eugenic religion that focused on manipulating the sexual behaviours of its inhabitants. The whole society was dedicated to breeding fitter and smarter humans for the betterment of the race, thus improving human life in ways barely dreamed of prior to that time. It was Galton's hope that his novel would spread these ideas even further among members of the wider population.

Despite his great hopes, Galton did not live to see the fruition of authoritarian eugenic policy. And publishers showed little interest in his novel. Indeed, it was not published in his lifetime, and most of it was destroyed after his death by his daughter, perhaps due to its odd passages about sexual reproduction. But authoritarian eugenics did reach its logical endpoint just a mere few decades after Galton's death. How it turned out, though, would be quite different to Galton's utopian vision. For even though eugenic ideology had been devised in England and expanded in America, it was in Germany, following the rise of Hitler and national socialism, that it was finally implemented on an industrial scale.

Born in 1889 in Austria-Hungary, Hitler was a strange child, full of resentment at others and seemingly unable to acknowledge his own inadequacies. He started out as a rather mediocre artist, studying in Vienna. Driven by his anti-Semitism and authoritarian nature, he was also increasingly drawn towards the new fascist politics that were emerging in Italy. At base, this was a petty-bourgeois movement that arose as a response to social crises of capitalism, and which then swung Italy and Germany towards imperialist reaction rather than towards revolution. This included further developing and implementing eugenic policy, this time on an industrial scale.

Hitler himself wrote on a range of eugenic and racist ideas before becoming leader of the National Socialist German Workers' Party in 1921. Driven by the ideologies of nationalism, racism, and eugenics, he eventually came to see society itself as an organism. In this view, a society's individual members were understood as either stronger or weaker, compared to each other on a more or less Galtonian model. And because society itself was an organism, the weaker individuals were seen as weakening the whole organism, while the stronger members were seen as strengthening it. Those who were seen as unable to conform to Nazi racial and economic requirements – those whose minds and bodies fell outside the norm – were thus essentially seen as parasitic problems to be eliminated.

Given these views, following Hitler's election as Chancellor in 1933 and the establishment of his dictatorship shortly after, the Nazi Party began implementing authoritarian eugenic laws and policies. This included the 'Law for the Prevention of Hereditarily Diseased Offspring' of 1935, which prescribed compulsory sterilisation for thousands of neurodivergent people including those diagnosed with schizophrenia and cognitive disabilities. In turn, the Aktion T4 campaign between 1939 and 1945 went further, focusing on the mass murder of people deemed to impede the overall organismic functioning of the race.

In retrospect this was all, quite clearly, based on racist and eugenicist ideology. Yet in many cases at the time the elimination was taken to be scientifically legitimised through Galtonian research methods and frameworks. For instance, as the historian Robert Proctor has detailed, research drawing on Galton's twin studies technique was 'lavishly funded' and 'purportedly demonstrated the heritability of everything from epilepsy, criminality, memory, and hernias to tuberculosis, cancer, schizophrenia, and divorce'.[11] New Galtonian psychometric and psychological methods were also used to determine who was weaker or stronger and thus who should be able to live and reproduce.

In practice this helped justify how mentally ill and intellectually disabled children and adults were classified, assessed, sterilised, and, in many cases, murdered in huge numbers alongside Jews and other targets of Nazi eugenic policy. For instance, up to 269,500 people with schizophrenia alone are thought to have been sterilised or murdered in Germany between 1939 and 1945.[12] Mothers of cognitively disabled children were told they were 'useless eaters', while doctors were required to report congenital impairments ranging from deafness to Down's syndrome. As Robison[13] notes, parents 'were encouraged to place those children in residential clinics, for the good of the family and the state. Once institutionalized, the children were systematically killed by poison, starvation, or exposure'. This was framed by Nazi doctors and politicians as a matter of 'racial hygiene' and as necessary for lifting the 'national burden' that the Nazi Party associated with disability.

Indeed, it was in Nazi-occupied Austria that autism was coined as a diagnosis. While the term had been coined by the eugenicist and psychiatrist Eugene Bleuler in 1911, Bleuler only meant it to refer to a temporary symptom of schizophrenia. It was only under Nazi rule, in the work of Hans Asperger in the 1930s and 1940s, that those who came to be called autistic were singled out as having a unique way of being. During a war period where men were expected to express a 'soldier mentality' and to be part of the group, boys who failed to fit this economic requirement were singled out as pathological (it was mostly boys who got the diagnosis) and were baptised with a new name: autism. Those women who were diagnosed were also singled out if they had intellectual disabilities, since they were not seen as fit to reproduce. Hence it was in significant part Nazi gender norms, determined by ideological and economic factors, that first allowed the autism spectrum to manifest as a distinct way of being.[14] In this context Hans Asperger and other medics began dividing autistics up into those deemed to have potential worth to the Third Reich given their purportedly strong logical capacities, and those who were to be sterilised or killed along with countless other mad and disabled targets.

These earlier eugenics policies have been described as 'the first chapter' of the Holocaust, where around 6 million Jews were murdered in line with Nazi racial ideology.[15] This was only halted by the allied victory in 1945. Prior to this, many British and American eugenicists had watched the eugenic experiment of Nazi Germany with great interest. But as the full extent of the horrors of the Holocaust increasingly came to light, support for authoritarian eugenic policies sharply declined in liberal societies. At the same time, Kraepelinian biological psychiatry also came to be seen as tainted through its association with Nazi eugenics. Because of this, Freudian psychoanalysis and behaviourism – the main alternatives to biological psychiatry available at the time – became dominant in US and European psychiatry in the 1950s. It is to these, and in turn the critique from anti-psychiatry critics, that we shall turn in the following chapters.

THE PATHOLOGY PARADIGM

I have outlined the intellectual and social history surrounding the mental health and normality concepts up until the mid-twentieth century. In theories of health, the core shifts I have detailed are the move from equilibrium to normal state conceptions of health and the Galtonian fusing of Darwin and normality to begin ranking populations. This happened within the rise of capitalism, which brought new cognitive hierarchies and accumulation of wealth by those whose cognitive dispositions fit this new mode of economic organisation. At the same time, new statistical methods and the mechanistic understanding of the body and mind allowed this to be scientifically legitimised.

The core assumptions of the pathology paradigm are that mental and cognitive functioning are individual and based on natural abilities, and can be ranked in relation to a statistical norm across the species. And while there were earlier notions of the mean understanding and normal body, I locate Galton as the founder of the pathology paradigm proper. Walker describes the pathology paradigm as being the place where the neurotypical mind became 'enthroned as the "normal" ideal against which all other types of minds are measured'.[16] And it was also with Galton that this, and mass normalisation, was formalised.

I also want to be clear here that, although I have focused on authoritarian eugenics, I do not mean to claim that eugenic theory is synonymous with pathology paradigm theory. As we have seen, Galton developed the basis of the paradigm several decades before he came up with the further notion of eugenics. Thus, while they are closely intertwined and grew together, they are not identical. The difference is that the pathology paradigm does not necessarily commit to the idea that the race or species can be improved at the group level. It only shares the underlying idea that we can rank populations in terms of mental abilities, and that higher in the ranking is more desirable. They are, then, closely interrelated but also distinct. This is important to recognise because there are countless, more or less subtle, ways this theory and ideology manifests in the Empire of Normality, and yet which are not based on an explicit attempt to improve the race or species. In fact, following the allied victory, many eugenics professors and researchers simply switched departments or roles, but carried on much as before. 'Eugenics' became 'genetics', for instance, and still focused on eliminating abnormalities even if this was framed as an individual medical problem more than an issue of race.

Indeed, as we shall see in the following chapters, a new Fordist, and then neoliberal, ideology of normality that became dominant in the twentieth century fused with later iterations of the pathology paradigm across a variety of sciences. While these would not, in most cases, be based on any conscious quest to improve the race, they would still be grounded in the same metaphysical assumptions as the earlier pathology paradigm. As such they would continue to reify even more restricted cognitive hierarchies that would manifest as capitalism continued to intensify and develop.

5

The myths of anti-psychiatry

One impact of Nazism was that a great many Jews and other targets of Nazi ideology fled the European continent in the 1930s. This mass exodus included some who were or would go on to become leading artists, philosophers, or scientists, who went to Britain, the United States, and elsewhere. Our own story now turns to two such men who, separately, fled Europe due to the Nazi threat. When each emigrated in the late 1930s, one was then an already famous neurologist and therapist whose ideas would shortly come to dominate American psychiatry. The other was a then-unknown teenage student. Yet, in time, he would go on to be among the most influential critics of the former's approach. And in pursuing this he would help found the philosophy of a movement that would bring psychiatry itself to its knees in the 1970s.

The elder of the two was Sigmund Freud. Born in 1856 in the town of Freiburg, then part of the Austrian empire, Freud was brought up by his father, a modest wool merchant, and his mother, an intelligent and quick-witted housewife. Freud himself was a diligent student and thus able to train as a physician and neurologist at the University of Vienna. He then worked on a range of research projects after graduating. This included early experiments on the therapeutic effects of cocaine and hypnosis. But it was his development of 'psychoanalysis' that brought his lasting fame. This was a theory and method for analysing what Freud called the 'unconscious' mind, which Freud used to develop a 'talking cure' for neuroses of the psyche. It was this that would later become a dominant school in psychiatry and psychology across much of the world.

The younger of the two, Thomas Szasz, never met Freud, but spent much of his life grappling with the former's thought and work. Born in 1920 in Budapest in what had then just become the Kingdom of Hungary to an upper-middle-class family, Szasz was brought up by his father, who ran a thriving agricultural business, his mother, and his governess. This was, at least, until the family had to flee the rise of Nazism to the US in 1938. Szasz was thus 18 when he moved across the Atlantic, just as Freud was living out his final months in London. And so it was in America that Szasz would study medicine, build a life, and, in time, become among psychiatry's most influential critics.

Today, although much of his work is now rejected, Freud is known as the father of psychoanalysis and psychotherapy. He is also a major figure in the history of psychiatry and psychology. By contrast, Szasz is known as the most influential of all 'anti-psychiatrists'. While he rejected the term himself, 'anti-psychiatry' is usually used to refer to a group of rogue psychiatrists and social theorists who challenged psychiatric pathologisation in the 1960s and 1970s. These included Ronald Laing, the Scottish psychiatrist who argued that schizophrenia is a reasonable reaction to distressing family dynamics, the Canadian sociologist Erving Goffman, who described asylums as 'total institutions' and diagnoses as 'labels', and the French philosopher Michel Foucault, whose work we have already mentioned.

While Szasz and Freud differed fundamentally in many commitments, they nonetheless shared a great deal beyond their religious background and profession. Both became influential for the counter-cultural movements in the late 1960s. They each also developed important theories relating to the mind, mental health, and society at large. Indeed, the ideas or arguments of each have also become so influential they are echoed daily today, often by people who are barely aware of their origins. And they have also each been part of an ongoing mass conflict between the state and those deemed mentally ill or disabled. To understand this, it is thus to Freud, Szasz, and the broader movements they are symbolic of, that our story now turns.

THE FREUDIAN TRIUMPH

As discussed in the previous chapter, Kraepelinian biological psychiatry was widely seen as tainted in liberal circles following increased awareness of the Holocaust. Eugenicists slunk away to genetics and psychology departments and rebranded their work without reference to the improvement of races. By contrast, Freud was Jewish and had thus fled from Vienna to England to escape persecution from the Nazis, who had detested his work given their anti-Semitism. As such his work was not tainted by an association with Nazism. Moreover, during a period of mass collective trauma, Freud's work was also useful for understanding the kind of psychological damage that followed the horrors of the Second World War. For instead of examining brains and using statistical analyses, Freud was interested in human suffering and how it might be explained in relation to unconscious drives, trauma, or early childhood experiences.

Indeed, not only was the Freudian approach seemingly useful for healing psychological problems. It was also useful for understanding society more broadly, as Freud himself first demonstrated in his 1929 book *Civilization and its Discontents*, where he examined the tension between the societal need for conformity and the individual sexual and aggressive instincts. Building on this, in a seminal 1933 book titled *The Mass Psychology of Fascism*,[1] Freud's follower Wilhelm Reich argued that Freudian theory might also be able to explain the rise of totalitarianism. Some thus came to believe that psychoanalysis might even help the rest of the world avoid repeating the horrors of the Holocaust. Others still, such as Freud's nephew and the father of public relations, Edward Bernays, drew on Freud's theories to help sell products and influence public perception. Bernays unashamedly defended what he described as the scientific development of 'propaganda' methods, which was helpful for capitalists and governments alike. Given such developments – alongside behaviourism, as we will see – the Freudian approach was able to quickly become a leading model in psychology and psychiatry. This was for understanding not just mental illness, but also child development and the human psyche much more broadly.

When it came to psychiatry, while there were only a small number of immigrant psychoanalysts in the United States in 1940, the Freudian approach would become the dominant school by 1950. Psychoanalysts came to run most university psychiatry departments, and psychoanalytic theory quickly came to influence other fields as well as art and culture. At the same time, partly after having dropped a nuclear bomb on Hiroshima, the United States was also undeniably the new world superpower. This power was in turn greatly increased in 1948, when the US donated over 13 billion dollars to help rebuild much of Europe and Turkey in exchange for increased influence and economic dominance. As such the scientific and cultural influence of US psychiatry was increasingly significant as the old European empires crumbled. Given the heightened influence of American imperialism, psychoanalysis established an at least temporary hegemony not just in the US but also far beyond.

Interestingly, while he did rely on Darwin for his understanding of instincts and drives, to some extent Freud briefly brought back aspects of an equilibrium conception of mental health. This is because – likely inspired by similar ideas from Ancient Egypt – Freud saw mental illness as stemming from the upset equilibrium between conscious and unconscious drives. For instance, certain drives might be repressed due to societal pressures or as a result of traumatic experiences, in ways that led to internal disharmony and thus psychic suffering. In making this move Freudian psychoanalysis and its offshoots brought great insights that had been missed in biocentric approaches. These were mainly regarding the workings of the psyche, the role of unconscious drives and instincts, and on the matter of childhood development and interpersonal dynamics.

This also brought a new therapeutic approach. Freud himself spent much time with patients helping them talk through their problems, hoping to untangle their internal conflicts. He then reported on and analysed these cases in his writings, which were widely read among clinicians and members of the educated public alike. In time, the Freudian approach came to help many suffering people, by introducing new frameworks and vocabularies alongside talking therapies that allowed people to confront traumas, help make sense of early childhood problems, and work through strained family relationships.

Despite Freud's great insights, the dominance of his followers was not destined to last. It was not just that many of his followers became dogmatists in their teaching and practice, especially after Freud's death in 1939. And neither was it just that the efficacy of psychoanalytic intervention had not been established through rigorous scientific testing. While these were genuine problems, it was also that Freud himself had broadened the boundaries of mental illness in such a way that ended up helping psychiatry expand its sphere of control. In his 1906 book *The Psychopathology of Everyday Life*, for instance, Freud suggested that pretty much *everyone* was somewhat neurotic, and that this could be detected in ordinary things such as forgetting words or unintended movements.[2] This meant that the psychoanalyst was now placed to heal a great variety of problems previously considered part of the ordinary suffering of daily life, and more the domain of the priest than the medic.

Alongside this broadening and blurring of the boundaries between the worried well and the unwell, many American psychoanalytic psychiatrists later overtook the running of the asylums without reforming them. Many barbarous practices and abuses continued much as before. And so for critics of the asylums, psychoanalysts became complicit in an existing state carceral system. At the same time, it was becoming increasingly apparent that patriarchal, racialised, and heteronormative power relations manifested in who was deemed mentally ill as well as how their problems were interpreted. Women were pathologised as 'hysterical' for challenging patriarchy, while Black men and women were labelled as having a 'protest psychosis' for resisting racism. Critics of this system began to analyse the conceptual and scientific basis of psychoanalysis itself, and to argue that it lacked sound scientific grounding or evidence.

By the end of the 1960s psychiatric survivors, health professionals, researchers, patients, and members of the broader public would thus end up becoming increasingly sceptical of Freudian psychiatry. In time, all this disquiet came to be captured in the anti-psychiatry movement, which – especially through the work of Szasz – brought a fierce critique of not just psychoanalytic psychiatry, but also of the very concept of 'mental illness' upon which they took psychiatry's power to be founded.

SZASZ ON THE 'MYTH' OF MENTAL ILLNESS

To understand this in more detail, let us return to 1938 – one year prior to Freud's death – when Szasz arrived in the United States. Once settled, Szasz studied physics and then medicine at the University of Cincinnati, graduating at the top of his class. Even as a student, Szasz later reported, he was already sceptical that psychiatry was a genuine branch of medicine. As a committed libertarian he was also firmly against involuntary confinement and much of what went on in the asylums.

Despite his reservations, Szasz initially wanted to be an independent psychoanalyst. While he did not see psychoanalysis as a branch of science or medicine, he made a sharp distinction between what he called 'consensual psychoanalysis' and 'pseudo-medical psychoanalysis'. The former, in his own words, was a kind of 'confidential dialogue that often helps people resolve their personal problems and may help them improve their ability to cope'.[3] By contrast, 'pseudo-medical psychoanalysis' wrongly purported to be a scientific intervention and was used to justify locking patients up against their will.[4] This latter approach, which positioned clients as patients in need of treatment, was seen by Szasz as a form of social control masquerading as science.

Szasz may not have believed psychiatry was a medical science, but he nonetheless had to complete his medical training to qualify to practice private psychoanalysis. He thus took up a psychiatry residency at Cincinnati General Hospital and then worked for several further years at the Chicago Institute for Psychoanalysis. During this period, he kept his views about psychiatry quiet in the knowledge that speaking out could damage his career prospects. Following this he joined the State University of New York as a professor in 1956, where he would work for the rest of his career. This also gave him the stability needed to begin writing, and in time, start publishing his critique of psychiatry.

To his students and colleagues, he quickly became known as a charismatic lecturer with a sharp wit. But he only achieved fame – or notoriety – with his 1960 article 'The Myth of Mental Illness', which he developed into a best-selling book of the same title the following year. While he had published a more minor critique several years earlier, it was here that his iconoclastic analysis of his own profession, and, implicitly, many of his former mentors and his current colleagues, was unleashed. These early works outlined the core arguments that he continued to develop for the rest of his life, and which have underpinned much critique of psychiatry since this time.

Szasz's argument[5] had a historical aspect and a philosophical aspect, and it will be useful to consider both. His historical claim was that 'mental illness' was a metaphor, proposed in the 1800s, that, over time, psychiatry had come to forget was a metaphor. Given this error, psychiatry had come to respond to mental illness as if it was a genuine medical issue. First, they thus tried to locate and treat it in the brain, even though there was no evidence that most mental illnesses were biologically grounded. In turn, they had conceptualised talking therapies as if they were medical, when in fact they were nothing more than forms of social support. While this could sometimes be useful, Szasz argued, it had come to give psychiatrists an unjustified social positioning that allowed them to imprison people for crimes they had not even yet committed, and may not ever do so. As such, for Szasz, over time the idea of mental illness, and the various specific psychiatric diagnoses such as hysteria or schizophrenia, had come to legitimise psychiatry as a form of state control by bestowing it with a medical respectability it did not deserve.

In turn, Szasz's philosophical critique aimed to render the very concept of 'mental illness' incoherent and invalid. Importantly – and in stark contrast to subsequent neurodiversity proponents – Szasz did not challenge the concept of biological or neurological normality in his critique of mental illness. In fact, the assumption that the concept of biological normality was wholly scientific and objective precisely underpinned his critique. His argument was only against the 'mental' part of mental illness or disorder. He held that if there was no known neurological or otherwise biological abnormality underpinning the 'mental' problem, then the problem is not a medical problem, and is only a 'problem in living'.

Szasz's argument thus essentially rested on a comparison between what he took to be objective bodily medicine and value-laden psychiatry. In his own words, any legitimate 'concept of illness' standardly 'implies deviation from a clearly defined norm. In the case of physical illness the norm is the structural and functional integrity of the human body'.[6] In particular he took cellular pathology resulting from lesion as the archetypical form of medical abnormality. Because he saw the idea of the normal body to be timeless and objectively grounded, Szasz posited that somatic medicine and its conceptions of normality were 'free from wide differences of ethical value'.[7]

By contrast, he argued, what we call 'mental illness' was importantly different to bodily illness. This was because, he wrote, the 'norm from which deviation is measured whenever one speaks of a mental illness is a *psychosocial and ethical one*'.[8] That is, whether a psychiatrist thought someone was mad or not would essentially come down to their subjective judgement, not an objective biological test. Hence in this argument, we can see that psychoanalytic psychiatry was based on a myth – the myth that mental illness is genuine illness – because psychoanalytic judgements about illness are relatively lacking in objectivity when *compared to* judgement about normality in bodily medicine.[9]

THE POLITICS OF ANTI-PSYCHIATRY

It should be noted that Szasz's arguments – which he elaborated on in a range of books in the following decades – did not go unchallenged. His first book was incredibly controversial and brought swift retaliation from members of his own profession. For a start, he was quickly banned from teaching. And in turn his colleagues debated over whether he should be fired. When it came to his arguments, his more nuanced critics pointed out that his thinking rested on a range of untenable binaries between the body and mind, neurological and mental, problems in living and illness. This was not merely a theoretical issue either. Taking Szasz's analysis seriously would mean excluding conditions widely seen as helpful to recognise. For instance, since the pathophysiology of migraines and cluster head-aches is not well known, and their symptoms are 'mental', they would not count as genuine medical conditions worthy of support on Szasz's framework.

For that matter, many patients did (and still do) find it helpful to see their psychological problems as mental illness or disability. Many also found state and professional support useful – yet all this would be undermined if Szasz's views became widely accepted. Importantly, critique here came not just from patients but also came from other anti-psychiatrists. The Italian anti-fascist Franco Basaglia and his co-workers, who developed a dialectical materialist analysis to liberate inmates from the Trieste asylums and build a more humane mental health support system, rejected Szasz's position. For them, the denial of mental illness was obviously absurd. Unlike Szasz, the Basaglians worked with patients who had experienced extreme mental health problems, and who saw this as illness rather than mere ordinary distress. Similarly, the equally radical Socialist Patients Collective, active in West Germany in the 1970s, held that mental illness was an undeniable fact, albeit primarily caused by capitalist domination and oppression.

Despite the warnings of his Marxist critics, who saw Szasz's views as a highly reactionary denial of mental illness, Szasz's arguments quickly became influential. This was the case on the libertarian right, where Szasz himself sat, but also across the political spectrum. Anti-psychiatrists on the centre-left, such as Ronald Laing, and on the far-left, such as the communist David Cooper, sympathised with many aspects of Szasz's arguments and developed their own analyses of madness, often in dialogue with Szasz's work. Indeed, it was Cooper who coined the term 'anti-psychiatry' in 1967, which he used to group together Szasz with Laing and other rebel psychia-trists of the age.[10] While the broader anti-psychiatry movement had a diversity of views, Szasz's engaging writing, precise arguments, and powerful rhetoric helped his analysis become the dominant counter-narrative.

Especially in the late 1960s as many counter-cultural and civil rights movements sprung up across the United States and beyond, anti-psychiatry was widely embraced alongside movements focusing on feminism, gay rights, and Black civil rights. The renowned 1976 Dialectics of Liberation conference in London, for instance, brought together anti-psychiatrists such as Laing and Cooper with the New Left intellectual Herbert Marcuse, the pan-Africanist Stokely Carmichael, and many other leading radical thinkers of the age.[11] In turn, anti-psychiatry rhetoric and ideas were central to many of the uprisings and protests of 1968. By the early 1970s, as Michael Staub has written, 'it would no longer be required to acknowledge Szasz's name in connection with his ideas, so "universal" and accepted had they by this time become.'[12] This was to the extent of helping bring about what Staub describes as a 'revolution'[13] not just in cultural understanding but also in legal approaches relating to mental illness, not least since it followed from Szasz's arguments that the insanity defence was invalid.

We see this in popular fictional accounts that adopted and further popularised Szaszian themes. The 1975 film adaption of Ken Kesey's 1962 novel *One Flew Over the Cuckoo's Nest* was especially popular, to the point of winning all five major Academy Awards. Starring Jack Nicholson as the protagonist Randle McMurphy, the film opens with McMurphy being put in a mental hospital after pretending to be insane to avoid prison. He ends up in a ward full of friendly inmates dominated and intimidated by cold and calculating staff. After being abused and controlled, McMurphy organises resistance and a plan to liberate the patients. Yet upon being caught, he is lobotomised – a far worse fate than would likely have awaited him in prison. Here we see all the core aspects of Szasz's analysis: mental illness as an illusion, psychiatrists as unable to distinguish between genuine and false illness, and psychiatry as a form of social control masquerading as care.

It is important to stress that a key reason the Szaszian vision was able to become so influential was that most of the problems identified regarding the treatment of patients were all too real. The treatment of asylum inmates, for instance, was especially bad. Judi Chamberlin, an influential survivor activist, described one hospital as a 'prison' where there 'was no phone, visitors were allowed only twice a week, and the locked ward door opened with a buzzer'.[14] In many institutions patients were routinely denied basic human rights, tied up, and subjected to barbarous treatments such as lobotomy, whereby part of the brain was removed to make patients more docile. At the same time, psychiatrists regularly pathologised women as hysterical, Black civil rights protestors as psychotic, and queer people as inherently ill, in ways that reinforced and obscured deeply entrenched forms of social domination.

Thus, a great many activists and members of the public alike were – rightly – increasingly concerned with what they saw as psychiatric overreach that functioned as a form of social control, and which justified human rights abuses and oppressive systems. And Freudians, having expanded the boundaries of pathology as well as having taken over the running of the asylums, took much of the blame for this. In turn, regardless of its errors and oversimplifications, the analysis of anti-psychiatry proponents, aided by popular fictional portrayals, was widely taken to help make sense of understandable worries about psychiatry.

The outcome of this was that for many then – and still today – it came to seem that the core problem for the mad and disabled was not just psychiatry itself but also the very concept of 'mental illness', not to mention psychiatric diagnoses, upon which its power was taken to be grounded. And the practical implication of this, for Szasz and his followers, would be that all manifestations of mental illness should be recast as non-medical 'problems in living'. By invalidating 'mental illness' as a category for making sense of human suffering, the Szaszian project sought to undermine the conceptual root of psychiatric legitimacy. For they saw the social control of patients not as stemming from capital and the state, but rather from the very idea of mental illness itself.

THE CLOSING OF THE ASYLUMS

The effects of the support for anti-psychiatry were significant. We will come back to how it impacted our understandings of mental disorder later. For now, perhaps most importantly, by changing public perception, anti-psychiatry helped rapidly speed up a major shift that started in the 1950s: the closing of the asylums. While many inmates and their supporters had campaigned to close or reform the asylums since the nineteenth century, the anti-psychiatry proponents had more developed arguments that managed to change public perception significantly. In line with this tradition, for the more right-wing libertarian anti-psychiatrists such as Szasz in the United States and, albeit with a quite different analysis, the anti-fascist Franco Basaglia in Italy, the idea was that this would liberate these patients from the kinds of coercion and social control the mad and disabled had been subjected to since at least the eighteenth century. Hence as Andrew Scull writes, a 'curious political alliance supported the dissolution of the state hospitals. On the left, a fierce opposition to the incarceration of the mentally ill in places that resembled prisons or warehouses for the unwanted'. But then on 'the right, a libertarianism that hated the public provision of services of any sort, coupled with the promise of fiscal savings, made closure of state hospitals equally irresistible'.[15]

By the same token, the combination of popular books and acclaimed media portrayals brought simultaneous significant and widespread sympathy for the shift from asylum to 'community' care. The basic idea was that former inmates would return to their communities, and be supported to live at least relatively ordinary lives, free from coercion or control. Policies towards this shift began to be developed and implemented. By the end of the 1970s almost all the asylums had closed, with many old buildings sold off or left empty. In turn, many former inmates – some who had spent most of their lives inside the asylum walls – were released back into the communities from which they had originally come. Finally, it seemed to many proponents of the Szaszian approach, liberation was imminent.

And yet despite the great hopes of the anti-psychiatrists, it increasingly became clear that their influence had not brought anything like widespread liberation. It is true that some former asylum inmates did manage to successfully return to their communities. And in a select few areas, some clinicians developed workable alternatives, and the shift to community care went well. Most notably, in the city of Trieste in Italy, Basaglia and his co-workers did manage to develop an effective alternative for patients in the community.[16] Their system had no locked doors, and patients were closely supported by dedicated and caring staff.

But in most cases, including across much of Europe and the United States, the closing of the asylums often did little to help former inmates. As Peter Sedgwick chronicled from England in 1982:

In Britain no less than in the United States, 'community care' and 'the replacement of the mental hospital' were slogans which masked the growing depletion of real services for mental patients: the accumulating numbers of impaired, retarded and demented males in the prisons and common lodging-houses; the scarcity not only of local authority residential provision for the mentally disabled but of day centres and skilled social-work resources; the jettisoning of mental patients in their thousands into the isolated, helpless environment of their families of origin, who appealed in vain for hospital admission (even for a temporary period of respite), for counselling or support, and even for basic information and advice.[17]

Many former inmates struggled to find work, began using illegal drugs or entered criminalised professions and ended up in prison after breaking the law, much as Szasz had indicated was preferable. Indeed, as recent research by the historian Anne Parsons[18] has shown, following the asylum closures, the prison industrial complex began to grow massively. But now it mainly incarcerated not just the (often) white former inmates of asylums. Rather, it grew to incarcerate, in much greater numbers, mad or disabled Black people alongside mad or disabled white people.

Just as many younger inmates were shifted to prisons, many older inmates were shifted to the nursing home, where they were no freer than before. As Andrew Scull has chronicled:

Between 1963 and 1969 alone, the numbers of elderly patients with mental disorders living in nursing homes increased by nearly 200,000, from 187,675 to 367,586. By 1972, with some younger patients added to the mix, the mentally disturbed population housed in nursing and board-and-care homes had risen to 640,000, and two years later, it rose to 899,500.[19]

These nursing homes were carceral systems no less than the prisons or asylums were. Similar abuses as happened in the asylums also happened in the nursing homes, and sometimes the latter were even worse. Indeed, even when there is no abuse, recent research suggests that in nursing homes, newly admitted patients tend to both be younger and more likely to become long-term residents if they also have a mental illness.[20] In retrospect it thus becomes apparent that rather than liberating patients from social control, anti-psychiatry helped facilitate their shift from one kind of carceral system to others that were often no better than the asylums.

Indeed, as Scull[21] has further detailed, support for anti-psychiatry even turned out to be useful for many states that wanted to save money. Due to gains in human rights and welfare support, fiscal pressures on the state intensified from the 1960s, leading to the remaining asylums being seen by governments as an overly costly waste of finances and resources. In the US, much of the change came down to specific states making manoeuvres to transfer costs on to federal government.[22] Many older inmates were also moved to nursing homes for financial rather than clinical reasons, since this meant that states did not have to employ more staff at the asylums. In this, the Szaszian ideology turned out to be useful for the ruling class rather than helping to resist the dominant system.

At the same time, as we shall see in the following chapters, the increased availability of basic welfare support alongside new psychotropic drugs also made it more economically viable to close the last asylums, regardless of whether the available community support or alternative institutions would be sufficient for survival. If anything, this was especially enticing for governments following 1973, during which one of capitalism's routine crises brought a great economic recession and mass unemployment. Hence, it is true that as the counter-cultural movements of the late 1960s and 1970s arose, the critique from anti-psychiatry certainly turned public opinion against the asylums as well as the very concept of mental illness. But in significant part, the asylums were shut down one by one, alongside rhetoric about returning patients to the community, to cut costs. And Szaszian scepticism regarding the reality of mental illness turned out to be useful for justifying this.

SZASZ AND THE PATHOLOGY PARADIGM

It should be noted here that the relationship between asylum closure, homelessness, and imprisonment is not quite as simple as it may seem. As Liat Ben-Moshe[23] has convincingly argued, both homelessness and prison also generate mental illness rather than just being places where mentally ill people end up. She also notes that abolition for people with intellectual disability, which was led by different, non-Szaszian advocates, was more successful, with many more former inmates successfully returning to communities. Given this, for Ben-Moshe, we should beware of any discourse that makes it out as if the only options for people experiencing mental illness are either incarceration or homelessness. This is important, she stresses, so we can recognise that the problem was not the abolition of the state asylums *as such*.

Yet the fact remains that the most dominant form of Anglo-American anti-psychiatry – stemming from the work of Szasz – was misguided, and its politics failed to liberate its subjects. To understand the flaws in the anti-psychiatry analysis, it is helpful to consider the Marxist psychologist Peter Sedgwick, who was anti-psychiatry's most insightful critic at the time. For Sedgwick, a big part of the issue was that Szasz's arguments were driven by and reproduced his hard-right libertarian politics. As Sedgwick pointed out, Szasz's worldview was hyper-individualistic. For him, every individual had complete responsibility and freedom, and he believed the state should leave people to make their own decisions in every aspect of life. Szasz himself was quite open that this view had been a consistent driver of his work from the beginning, and he even wrote letters to the 'father' of neoliberalism, the economist

Friedrich Hayek. In their correspondence he proudly identified as Hayek's 'disciple' and emphasised how his critique of psychiatry was influenced by his Hayekian worldview.[24]

In particular, this world view underpinned Szasz's belief that people self-identified as 'mentally ill' mainly to take on a 'sick role' that allowed them to avoid taking personal responsibility for dealing with their problems in living. Liberal capitalists had long been worried about so-called 'malingerers' – people pretending to be ill to avoid responsibility – and the Hayekian philosophy perhaps entrenched this even further, as it centred the individual beyond all else. Essentially, then, Szasz saw patients as morally weak liars, pretending to be ill, rather than unwell people in need of medical assistance. For Szasz, the 'myth' of mental illness was as much a myth made and sustained by patients as it was made by psychiatrists. As he wrote in his 2008 book *Psychiatry: Science of Lies*, 'So-called mentally ill persons' all in fact 'pretend to be disabled by illnesses that do not exist'.[25]

While many patients who were wrongly pathologised found Szasz's analysis useful, then, the ultimate implication of accepting it was not only that state support and psychiatric diagnosis should be abolished, even for those who found them helpful. It was also that claiming to be mentally unwell was really a form of lying, to oneself and others, in order to avoid responsibility for dealing with life's problems. More concretely, if someone commits a crime in a state of psychosis, and if the crime followed from their actions, they should be punished by community or state no less than someone who committed the same crime in a cold and calculating manner. It was not, then, an accident that Szasz's arguments implied that the insanity defence was invalid. Rather, it was his concerns relating to individual responsibility that drove his theorising about mental illness.

In this the Szaszian project would seek to go back to a pre-medical, and much more conservative, world view, where what we now call mental illness would be understood in the moral rather than medical sphere. From the Szaszian perspective, then, the shift from asylum to prison incarceration was a desired outcome, not an unfortunate side-effect. In other ways, his politics also anticipated the neoliberalism that would begin being imposed from around 1979. After all, according to Hayek modern shifts towards collectivism from the left had become soft and thus, in his own words, the virtues of 'independence, self-reliance, and the willingness to bear risks' were now 'less esteemed and practiced'.[26] It was, arguably, not just Hayekian neoliberalism but also such a narrative of moral decline that Szasz took up in suggesting that modern people were worse at dealing with life. It was this that allowed him to see all mental health patients as malingerers who had developed a new concept – that of mental illness – to avoid having to take responsibility for their behaviours. And part of why this was so widely attractive is that it fits with a broader form of capitalist individualism that would culminate in the global adoption of Hayek's politics in the 1980s.

Alongside this, Sedgwick also noted that Szasz and many other anti-psychiatrists relied on a depoliticising and reified notion of bodily normality in order to make their claim that psychiatry was comparatively unscientific. Szasz, most clearly, built his argument based on the assumption that bodily medicine dealt with objective abnormalities of the body, as if bodily normality were a timeless fact, which he then compared to a comparatively 'mythical' mental illness. Yet Sedgwick contended that conceptions of bodily illness were also no less value-laden than those of mental illness – a claim that is well supported by what we have covered in this book already in the previous chapters. It is not just that many bodily conceptions of normality are also contested – for instance, the use of Quetelet's Body Mass Index to determine the so-called normal weight – it is also that the very idea of bodily normality, and the specific standards now used, are the product of specific social and material conditions. They are and remain intimately intertwined with racist, patriarchal, and capitalist logics. The Szaszian view, by contrast, precisely needs to downplay the ideological nature of bodily conceptions of normality, in order to be able to posit that conceptions of mental illness are so unlike those used in general medicine.

In this regard, Sedgwick also critiqued what he called 'psycho-medico dualism' underlying the Szaszian analysis. Szasz's position was essentially Cartesianism taken to its extreme and applied to the understanding of mental health. For the precise combination of a wholly mechanistic understanding of the body as a working or broken machine, with a sharp dualism to preserve the sanctity of the mind, is unambiguously reminiscent of the distinction we have seen Descartes make in his *Meditations* over three centuries earlier. And just as with Descartes' own work, Szasz's contained both the same conceptual problems while also turning out to be incredibly useful for capital. This time, though, it was not the industrialists and slave owners of the old European empires, but the neoliberal politicians of the late twentieth century, who would find it so helpful. By the 1980s, it had become clear to critics such as Sedgwick that Szaszianism was mostly convenient for framing unwell people as work-shy malingerers, and thus for justifying cuts to services and welfare.

Finally, the basis of Szasz's view is that the correct functioning of the mechanistic body is precisely *normal* functioning. For him, health was equated with the functional and structural normality of the body. As he took this to simply be an objective and natural normative standard, he fully bought into the underlying logics of the pathology paradigm. He might superficially look like he challenged it, because he proposed that mental illness was not real illness. But this is really just the most sharply dualistic manifestation of the pathology paradigm, rather than an alternative to it.

Overall then – despite many anti-psychiatrists bringing important insights into how psychiatry functioned as a form of social control – the most influential anti-psychiatry analyses missed the target. Many of the anti-psychiatrists believed that the 'myth' of mental illness and psychiatric 'labels' were the core problems. They were what Marx called *idealists*, taking the power of psychiatric control to come from belief in the ideas of psychiatry. And so they thought that denying the reality of mental illness, reducing mental illnesses to mere 'labels', and closing the asylums would liberate patients. But in fact, as a materialist analysis shows, conceptions of mental illness and psychiatric diagnoses were not where the power guiding this social control lay. Rather, the ways these institutions and practices often harmed people were only specific manifestations of the broader neuronormative logics of the capitalist system. Because of this, capital was able to use anti-psychiatry's denial of the reality of mental illness and suspicion of psychiatric diagnosis to shift the mad and disabled from one form of social control to others. These were often no less bad and were sometimes worse.

Part of what the anti-psychiatry movement shows us, looking back, is perhaps that capital requires us to recognise mental illness just enough to maintain a surplus class, but not enough for it to be forced to grant recognition and sufficient support where it is costly. And the debate between psychiatrists and anti-psychiatrists, which led to a false dichotomy between seeing mental illnesses as apolitical diseases or mere myths, helped maintain this equilibrium rather than challenging it. Thus, despite the mass energy harnessed by the anti-psychiatry movement, most of those to be locked away never really escaped, while many of those who wanted help never received it. And so capitalism and the pathology paradigm were able to continue their development relatively unhindered.

6

Fordist normalisation

Anti-psychiatry brought two contributions. First, a seminal analysis of psychiatric social control that helped resist certain manifestations of psychiatric oppression. Second, it brought new grounds for a cultural denial of mental illness that helped provide the state with a way to save money by closing the asylums while shifting former inmates to other carceral systems. This has since had a significant and lasting impact on the politics of mental health, as will be explored in more detail below. But to understand what really happened in this period, and to see more clearly why closing the asylums did not lead to liberation for the mad and disabled, we again need to turn to the ongoing development of capitalism. After all, more general shifts in broader material conditions and technologies that were underway while Szasz was still in training were already paving the way for new neuronormative practices to take hold. This would allow an alternative field, clinical psychology, to develop new methods and techniques for care and control that purported to be more effective than anything the Freudians had to offer.

Two economic factors following the Second World War are of particular importance. The first is the rise of the welfare capitalism championed by the economist Keynes, who we have already mentioned considering his role in the Eugenics Society. The second is the rise of the Fordist economic model, and with it the development of new Fordist technologies of care and control that could be used beyond the walls of the asylum. As we shall see, these broader economic shifts would bring not just new forms of intervention, but also new technologies and a tightening of neuronormativity in relation to the developing needs of capital. This would lead to a much greater portion of the population coming to be considered abnormal, far more than could be housed in state-funded asylums. They would instead be subject to new forms of intervention that extended far beyond the locked doors of the increasingly obsolete state hospitals. This would now start from the earliest years of life, and would increasingly expand through school, the workplace, and, finally, in the minds and behaviours of the population at large.

FORDISM

To understand this, we need to go back to the 1910s and 1920s, when Henry Ford, an industrialist based in Detroit, had pioneered a new economic model. Born in 1863 in Michigan to a family of farmers, Ford gained a reputation as a watch repairer in his teenage years before moving to Detroit to become an apprentice machinist and then engineer while he experimented with gasoline engines in his spare time. By 1901, he was able to start his own company, the Ford Motor Company, where he would manage not just great feats of engineering but also a new model of manufacturing.

Ford invented the assembly line, thus developing what came to be known as assembly line manufacturing. However, this work was too harrowing and alienating for workers to stay long in the job without good pay. Ford was thus forced to offer high wages and good welfare to retain the best employees. He then used these employees to mass produce standardised goods that could be sold at low prices and in large numbers. Simultaneously, he also established a monopoly in advertising in Detroit publications before doing the same nationally. This led to his Ford cars becoming the standard across the United States. This economic model went against the conventional wisdom of the capitalists of the time, who generally paid the lowest wages possible. It also went against the logic of the automobile industry, which had produced cars as luxury products to sell in small numbers at high prices.

Yet Ford's model turned out to be incredibly successful, making him exceptionally rich and leading to the widespread use of cars as the primary form of transport in the United States. His model was so successful, in fact, that it led to ushering in the new form of assembly line manufacturing and mass marketing that would quickly become the dominant model. It was emulated not just across the United States but far beyond. Even in Nazi Germany, for instance, after hearing about Ford's success, Hitler personally demanded that Volkswagen find a way to mass produce affordable cars on a Fordist model. It was this that led to the development of the Volkswagen Beetle, which turned out to be even cheaper, and in time, better selling than any of Ford's cars long after Hitler and Nazi Germany had been consigned to history. Similar innovations were quickly developed elsewhere, leading to a new form of work and the furthering of scientific work management for hard, monotonous jobs.

The ascent of Fordism took place alongside the adoption of Keynesian economics in the United States and the United Kingdom following the Second World War. While he was certainly no Marxist, Keynes nonetheless held that a healthy economy required not cutting and saving, but, rather, stimulating more demand and more spending. In a time where capitalist governments and policymakers were worried about communist sympathies, this approach was seen as a good way to appease the working classes and fend off the spread of communism. Keynes was a key designer of the Bretton Woods conference of 1944 where dozens of governments met to agree on a new post-war exchange system. This essentially pegged the value of gold to the US dollar, helping solidify US supremacy, and it also led to the founding of the International Monetary Fund and the World Bank. Keynesian thinking thus guided the post-Second World War trading system across much of the capitalist world.

In turn, during the 1950s and 1960s Keynesian government investment at the state level alongside the ascent of Fordism brought a great economic boom. States were spending more and so were workers, and a great many people could afford new goods that were previously reserved only for the wealthy. In this period, many ordinary people had high-paid jobs and were thus able to achieve a quality of life that would have been barely imaginable by their parents or grandparents. At the same time, welfare, in terms of government benefits, healthcare, and so forth, even increased for those who couldn't work. The fusing of Fordist and Keynesian approaches thus brought about the so-called 'Golden Age' of capitalism, including modern welfare systems, education, and services.

While this improved the lives of many, it also brought a new form of alienation relating to the capitalist manufacturing of 'normal' desires for consumers alongside restricted norms for employment and work. The production of false needs had already been observed by Karl Marx who had written as far back as 1857 that, to the capitalist, the 'total mass of all workers' appeared as potential consumers, and thus that capitalists constantly needed to search 'for means to spur' consumers 'on to consumption'.[1] While this had already begun in Marx's time, the capacity for capital to manufacture desire grew significantly in the twentieth century, while the pressure to do so rose with the need to sell their wares to ever-growing numbers of consumers. After all, on the Fordist model, it no longer was the point to sell luxuries to the rich but rather to sell standardised products to the masses. This would increasingly bring the normative demands of capital out of the workplace and into individual and collective psyches.

It was Freud's cousin Edward Bernays who most forcefully defended the adoption of these methods by governments in liberal democracies to control the desires of their populations. Building on his earlier explanation and defence of propaganda, in 1947 he published an essay titled 'The Engineering of Consent' in the *Annals of the American Academy of Political and Social Science*. Here Bernays clarified how, in his own words, 'the engineer of consent must create news. News is not an inanimate thing. It is the overt act that makes news, and news in turn shapes the attitudes and actions of people'.[2] By this time, Bernays himself had been incredibly successful at manufacturing false needs, being most well known at the time for having used such methods to help tobacco companies convince women to take up smoking in much greater numbers in a 1929 advertising campaign. But now he defended the method not just for the marketing of goods, but for the control of the populations by the state.

From a more critical perspective, the rise of such methods was examined in real time by the Frankfurt School critical theorists

Max Horkheimer and Theodor Adorno in their 1946 book *Dialectic of Enlightenment*. As Jewish intellectuals on the left, they had fled the Nazis and emigrated to the United States in the 1940s. Yet when they arrived, they found themselves increasingly horrified at what they saw as a mass restriction on free thought that made the United States little freer than Nazi Germany. Among other factors, they argued that the mass production of false needs and desires had increased following the rise of mass media and public relations alongside standardised products. For instance, the invention of the radio, they wrote, made 'everyone equally into listeners, in order to expose them in authoritarian fashion to the same programs put out by different stations'. This brought, they went on, 'a cycle of manipulation and retroactive need' to unify 'the system ever-more tightly'.[3] While the idealised average consumer did not actually exist, each person did sit closer or further to this ideal, or was thus more or less prone to adopting those desires demanded by the profit margins of new giant companies that utilised variants of the Fordist model.

It was also this that Herbert Marcuse, one of the leading figures of the New Left, examined in his 1964 book *One-Dimensional Man*. For Marcuse the mass production of Fordist goods alongside new marketing techniques had brought a new form of alienation that had not been present in earlier phases of capitalism. In his own words, while 'choice among a wide variety of goods and services' was presented as evidence of capitalism's deliverance of freedom to the masses, this in fact did not 'signify freedom if these goods and services sustain social controls over a life of toil and fear – that is, if they sustain alienation'.[4] In fact, for Marcuse, the monotony of Fordist work alongside the false promise of its consumerism led to psychological repression of a mass scale, unseen at any previous point in history. For him, at that time, society itself was making people psychologically unwell due to the tightness of the psychic dominance of capital and its demand for what he called 'surplus repression' of desires.

Simultaneously, as Harry Braverman explored in his 1974 book *Labour and Monopoly Capital*, a range of government reports in the United States and the United Kingdom from the time found that workers were becoming increasingly unsatisfied with work, were taking more sick days, and thus production levels were decreasing. On Braverman's analysis, the ever-increasing division of labour led to a deskilling among workers that made their jobs increasingly unfulfilling and alienating, even when compensated by better pay and increased access to new commodities. Unable to take pride in their monotonous work, people tended to feel unfulfilled despite access to a greater number of possessions than their parents and grandparents had had.

Thus, while the Golden Age of capitalism did improve the lives of many people – at least those living in wealthy, Western nations – in important ways, it also hindered their thriving in other ways. During a mass drive to push each person towards an idealised norm of desires in the post-war years, many of those who adopted these new desires often felt increasingly unfulfilled and alienated despite increased consumption – and those who fell outside were increasingly stigmatised and othered. In short, neuronormativity became more restricted, changing psychological expectations in relation to the needs not of humanity, but of capital itself.

BEHAVIOURIST NORMALISATION

In retrospect, we might add to Marcuse's analysis that, by contrast, those whose minds had further proximity from fitting with this new consumer normativity – increasingly became deemed problems to be fixed. We see the combined effects of these government and commercial efforts most clearly in the rise of child psychiatry and psychology, which had barely existed before the 1940s. As Nadesan writes, during the early twentieth century, the expanding 'interest in childhood "development" led to' new divisions of children based on 'their degree of apparent normality in relation to newly created and standardised developmental norms'.[5] This mirrored the rise of standardised schooling – which was expanded following the Second World War – not to mention Galtonian ideas about different kinds of innate intelligence. In this context, differences in development in comparison to one's age group became increasingly salient, and new notions of developmental 'milestones' brought more restricted standards of developmental normality.

But one reason the shift to Fordism is particularly important is that alongside restricting neuronormativity, it also brought new Fordist methods of care and control. Following the critique from anti-psychiatry, while costly psychoanalytic approaches, and the more barbaric treatments such as lobotomy, became less popular, new more economically efficient and lucrative therapeutic approaches were increasingly adopted and developed. In an important sense these would allow psychiatry and psychology to extend their reach far beyond the walls of the asylums, and into a much greater part of public and private life. Among the most important of these was *behaviourism*. This would be developed by psychologists, giving them increased clinical and societal influence that would in time come to match that of the psychiatrists of the asylums.

Pioneered by the psychologist John Watson, born in South Carolina in 1848, American behaviourism sought to overcome the divide between the mind and body that dated back at least to the work of Descartes, who had proposed a dualism between the soul and the mechanistic body. While the Cartesian tradition had left the mind unobservable and thus hard to study scientifically, by the 1910s Watson proposed the revolutionary idea that psychological science should focus only on what could be objectively observed: behaviour. By attending to behaviour alone he sought not only to provide psychology with new levels of respectability, but also to revolutionise the way psychologists carried out clinical work.

When it came to clinical intervention, Watson was inspired by the research of the Russian psychologist Ivan Pavlov. In the 1890s, Pavlov had found that dogs began salivating whenever they heard the footsteps of research assistants who routinely brought them their food.[6] Because of this, Pavlov had suggested that dogs could develop a 'conditioned' response, whereby they learned to react in a certain way to familiar stimuli based on past experiences. It was this that Watson believed could be applied to understanding and treating humans. In time, he came to believe that our behaviours such as speech, emotional responses, and so forth were simply the combination of our innate tendencies combined with repeated exposure to stimuli that then conditioned typical responses. As we will return to later, having been the first Russian Nobel laureate in 1904, Pavlov was praised by Lenin himself following the Russian revolution. As we will return to later, this combined with a new form of what Lenin called 'state capitalism' in Soviet Russia, which paralleled the rise of behaviourism in market capitalist societies.

In the West, Watson's theoretical work was incredibly influential, being championed by philosophers such as Bertrand Russell as well as inspiring psychologists and sociologists dissatisfied with Cartesianism. But it was his proposal that he could change behaviours through operant conditioning that had by far the greatest impact. In his influential 1924 book, simply titled *Behaviourism*, he wrote:

> Give me a dozen healthy infants, well-formed, and my own specified world to bring them up in and I'll guarantee to take any one at random and train him to become any type of specialist I might select – doctor, lawyer, artist, merchant-chief and, yes, even beggar-man and thief, regardless of his talents, penchants, tendencies, abilities, vocations and the race of his ancestors.[7]

In other words, Watson suggested that, regardless of heredity, he could mould infants to become certain kinds of people, or even to fit specific job roles. The potential of behaviourism thus lay in its promise to be able to mould individuals in line with the needs of the society and economy.

Influenced by Watson, a massive shift towards increasingly ambitious behaviourist research programmes soon began. By the 1930s, the Harvard psychologist B. F. Skinner began using behaviourist principles to mimic evolutionary selection pressures to change behaviours, including in those deemed mentally ill. Skinner's approach, as detailed in his 1938 book *The Behavior of Organisms*, used punishments or rewards as 'reinforcers' to make people better fit current societal requirements.[8] This grounded what he thought of as 'behavioural engineering', which could, he proposed, be used on a mass scale to produce desirable citizens. Indeed, a whole 'culture', he wrote in his later book *Beyond Freedom and Dignity*, 'is very much like the experimental space used in the analysis of behaviour. Both are sets of contingencies of reinforcement'. Given this, Skinner went on, designing 'a culture is like designing an experiment'.[9] By the same token, he claimed, improving a culture can be achieved through 'piecemeal' operant conditioning of its people to fit the needs of society at large.

This was important because it meant that Darwinists and policy makers, deprived of widespread support for Galtonian eugenics, now saw a new method for normalising populations. But this time it sought to mimic evolutionary pressures in childhood development rather than through control of hereditary traits across generations. In this context, as Harvard historian Rebecca Lemov has detailed,[10] large American philanthropic organisations such as the Rockefeller Foundation, which had previously funded Nazi eugenics, began lavishly funding new behaviouralist research. Most notably, this included the work of Elton Mayo, who sought to 'adapt industrial workers to their tasks by deradicalizing them through psychological counselling'.[11] This would formalise and update the kinds of scientific management that had been pioneered on slave plantations to manage the psyches of modern workers. Over this period, as Lemov writes, while the staff and trustees of such foundations 'had no dire or secret plan to rest democratic freedom-of-action or freedom-of-thought from average Americans', they nonetheless 'believed that the outside imposition of policies and of normality itself was necessary for the smooth functioning of any social system'.[12] As such, they saw investment in new forms of behavioural control as vital for the functioning and survival of American democracy itself.

Newer combinations of Freudianism and behaviourism became particularly influential during the Cold War, which began in 1945, as capitalist governments worried about how to stop people from sympathising with the other side. In the United States, for instance, Members of the Central Intelligence Agency were deeply concerned by reports that Maoist communists in the Far East had developed techniques of 'brainwashing' to make people support their cause.

This had first been reported by the anti-communist journalist Edward Hunter in a 1950 article in *Miami News*, which had the terrifying headline: 'Brain Washing Tactics Force Chinese into Ranks of the Communist Party'.[13] While there was little substance to Hunter's reports, the United States – terrified of communism spreading – soon began investing heavily in research into the uses of behaviourism, seeking to reverse engineer the so-called brainwashing techniques of the communists. Their basic idea, as Lemov writes, was to 'quantify and control the internal arena of the personal self – its urges and wants, its worries and fears' so governments could 'regulate human beings in tune with the needs, demands, desires, and models of the social order'.[14] In other words, the CIA and American government hoped that the techniques they believed were being used to increase sympathy for revolutionary communism could be co-opted and adapted to support the victory of capitalism. And the techniques they believed were being used were precisely the methods that had been developed by the behaviourists.

Simultaneously, especially since the Fordist period was defined by stable manufacturing and technical jobs, the role of behaviourism was increasingly seen to consist in how children might be shaped to fit one economic role they would keep for life. Importantly, it was not just psychologists who believed in such uses, but also industrialists including Henry Ford II, the grandson of Henry Ford I and the president and CEO of Ford Motor Company from the mid-1940s. As the sociologist and critic of behaviourism Daniel Bell observed in 1947,

> The Ford Motor Company announced a short while ago that it was setting aside $500,000 for research into 'human relations'. The company, Henry Ford II said, felt that it could go no further in the direction of technological rationalization of machines, and that the next step in engineering would have to be the raising of the level of 'human achievement'.[15]

Indeed, beyond the factories, Skinner even proposed that mass implementation of behaviourist principles could solve what he saw as the 'serious' issues of young people being reluctant to join the armed forces or of them wanting to work 'as little as possible'.[16]

This approach was built on how psychotherapeutic models had been used in the post-war Child Guidance Movement, which was led by eugenicists such as Cyril Burt, who we mentioned in Chapter 4. Proponents of the Child Guidance Movement had posited 'a spectrum of normalcy and the point at which any child might be located'[17] and had framed the childhood mind as uniquely susceptible to intervention that would aid workplace adjustment later in life. While this was initially built on more Galtonian assumptions, by the 1960s, such efforts had blended with the philosophy of the behaviourists, and thus behaviourism had started being used to enforce conformity for children who were considered pathologically subnormal.

Perhaps the most notable example of this is the method of Applied Behaviour Analysis, developed by Ivar Lovaas at the University of California in the 1960s. Lovaas agreed with Szasz that the concept of mental illness mainly functioned to help people evade responsibility. Instead of trying to heal people from 'illness', he thus instead sought to discipline them for what he saw as abnormal behaviours. His method used a harsh punishment and reward system to normalise 'abnormal' children. Autistic children were punished by Lovaas and his team through electric shocks or slaps every time they behaved in ways that seemed to reflect abnormal desires. As *Life* Magazine reported in a widely-read profile on Lovaas in 1965, the idea was to use operant conditioning on autistic children to 'push the child toward normality'.[18] Lovaas then used the same technique in the 1970s on boys considered too 'feminine', who were presumed to have 'homosexual' tendencies.[19] This was essentially a form of conversion therapy, which was initially thought to be successful but in fact led to long-term trauma.

Throughout this period, then, new norms of childhood reflected a broader shift derived both from the perceived capacity to work as well as the perceived ability to exhibit the correct desires and behaviours as consumers. Normality is restricted even further in relation to the shifting needs of capital, alongside other intersecting pressures from gender norms and heteronormativity. Thus in the post-war decades, it was not just that new forms of production brought new career prospects for aspirational workers: it was also that the production of normal children itself became a goal for aspirational and worried parents.

It is true that this development did certainly have its critics at the time. According to Bell, for instance, the new approaches pioneered by the likes of Elton Mayo, 'adjusted men to machines' in ways that 'introduced without any consideration of their ultimate and far-reaching effects' to humanity. But despite these critics, it was from this basis that behaviourism would go on to increasingly be embraced in a wide range of other areas, for instance in business to increase employee performance or in fitness industries to build desired eating and exercise habits, for instance, to push people towards Quetelet's notion of the ideal weight. It would also increasingly come to be combined with cognitive and psychoanalytic approaches to provide new targeted forms of intervention. This was much as the likes of Watson and Skinner had envisioned and would equally be in line with Kraepelin's notion of a 'mass psychiatry' he had proposed back in 1908.

FORDIST PHARMACEUTICALS

When it came to therapeutic intervention, an equally relevant major product of the Fordist era was the discovery and mass production of psychopharmacological drugs. This began in the 1950s and rapidly expanded in ways that radically changed how depression, anxiety, and psychosis were understood. As Robert Whitaker summarises, during this period:

Thorazine, Miltown, and Marsilid were all derived from compounds that had been developed for other purposes – for use in surgery or as possible 'magic bullets' against infectious diseases. Those compounds were then found to cause alterations in mood, behavior, and thinking that were seen as helpful to psychiatric patients. The drugs, in essence, were perceived as having beneficial *side effects*. [Seeing a new opportunity] psychiatry then reconceived the drugs as 'magic bullets' for mental disorders, the drugs hypothesized to be antidotes to chemical imbalances in the brain.[20]

In fact, studies of the drugs only evidenced limited efficacy and did not sufficiently document potential risks. Neither was there any evidence of a chemical imbalance underlying clinical depression or anxiety. Nonetheless, the drugs were easy to mass produce, and enough people found them useful for them to catch on. Indeed, anecdotally, many found and still find them literally lifesaving.

These new drugs were thus mass marketed to make increasingly huge profits for pharmaceutical companies and to provide support for struggling people. By 1954, 2 million Americans were taking chlorpromazine alone.[21] Following this, the numbers of psychiatric medications increased year after year, leading to a significant change in how depression and melancholy were understood. No longer were they reactions to traumatic events primarily treatable by expensive, personalised talking therapy; rather, they stemmed more from so-called 'chemical imbalances' – a vague term that allowed a great variety of interpretations, including for those marketing them – treatable by new standardised pharmaceuticals.

It should again be stressed that for some these new interventions were helpful, especially those who found the new drugs helped them manage psychosis, depression, or anxiety. Thus, in some instances, in the post-war decades, psychiatric and psychological interventions helped people suffering from mental health problems. But for many others, new forms of Fordist intervention brought new forms of social control. After all, the new drugs were mass-produced standardised products, and were not adapted to the specific needs, problems, and contexts of any individual's life. If the meds didn't work, patients would often be prescribed a heavier dose or a second medication, despite the increased risk of side effects and, in many cases, limited efficacy of this intervention. Because human neurodiversity and complexity were not accounted for by the logics of this approach, it could be experienced as a form of control in some cases even while it was experienced as vital care in others.

This further helps us understand the limitations of not just bio-medical psychiatry, but also the anti-psychiatry movement of the 1960s. As we saw in the previous chapter, while the asylums closed, new forms of normalisation expanded out into the community or shunted them towards the prison system or nursing homes. But as we have seen, just as importantly, for others still, they were controlled beyond the walls of any carceral system, by new Fordist technologies of normalisation. Thus, in the majority of cases, closing the asylums and ending psychoanalytic hegemony would not have liberated the mad or mentally ill as the anti-psychiatrists had hoped even if they had not been put in alternative carceral systems instead.

For in the Fordist period, society itself became both a laboratory and asylum for new behavioural and psychopharmacological interventions. And as the Freudian psychiatrists lost influence, the power vacuum left by them was filled by the new behaviourist psychologists intervening in childhood development right from the beginning of life, through education, and then in the workplace. For those who were harmed by this, the walls that trapped them were not made of brick and mortar but were psycho-technological, imposed by the increasingly strict behavioural reinforcers used by governments, psychologists, and public relations professionals. The anti-psychiatrists were, then, right that psychiatry often functioned as a form of social control. But in viewing the problem as relating to belief in the reality of mental illness, and in the abuses specific to the psychiatric asylums, it had missed the target. These were not in fact the core problems, but just one of the ways in which underlying problems often manifest. The true issue was not the mere concept of mental illness, but rather how increasingly restrictive conceptions of normality were produced and reproduced in line with shifting material conditions and relations. Despite the huge energy of the anti-psychiatry movement, capitalism was thus nonetheless able to continue its growth, and tighten its neuronormative grip, relatively undisturbed. It was in this context that Galtonian psychiatry would come to be reborn anew.

7

The return of Galtonian psychiatry

On a hot day in mid-July of 1990, United States President George H. W. Bush proclaimed the beginning of the 'Decade of the Brain'. For Bush, a 'new era of discovery' was dawning, whereby, in his words, 'Powerful microscopes, major strides in the study of genetics, and advances in brain imaging devices are giving physicians and scientists ever greater insight into the brain'. He went on to triumphantly espouse the merits of American psychiatry and neuroscience, before ending with a call for 'all public officials and the people of the United States to observe that decade with appropriate programs, ceremonies, and activities'.[1]

This moment did not come out of nowhere. To understand it, we need to turn back to consider one final major impact of the anti-psychiatry movement. This concerns the very concept of mental illness, which towards the end of the 1970s sharply shifted away from Freudian models and back towards biocentric models. This had in part been a response to critiques from anti-psychiatry critics. But a related crisis arose from what was then called 'homosexuality'. The pathologisation of queerness had initially been proposed long before, by the German psychiatrist Richard von Krafft-Ebing in his 1886 book *Psychopathia Sexualis*, which drew on Darwin to frame homosexuality as a form of psychopathology. Because reproduction was associated with fitness, same-sex attraction was seen as an impediment to natural functioning. Given the increasingly homophobic culture of the early twentieth century, and despite Freud himself seeing 'homosexuality' as non-pathological, this framing caught on.

At the same time, the American government had increasingly been collecting statistics on people with psychiatric conditions, to help with the social administration of populations. This programme had massively grown during the Second World War, when many military personnel were deeply traumatised only to be given overly vague and general diagnoses, while the government worried about malingerers. Early manuals developed by the US military to provide greater precision eventually were developed into the American Psychiatric Association's diagnostic bible, the *Diagnostic and Statistical Manual of Mental Disorders* or DSM, the first edition of which was published in 1952. While it only had limited impact in its first edition, its influence would increasingly grow over its many subsequent editions, and in time it would become one of the most influential books ever published.

In the DSM-I, which was influenced by the Freudian as well as biological approaches, 'homosexuality' came to be listed as a 'sociopathic personality disturbance'.[2] It was similarly included in the DSM-II, published in 1967, as a 'sexual deviation', around the same time Ivor Lovaas was developing his behaviourist conversion therapy already mentioned.[3] Throughout this period, gays and lesbians were increasingly subjected to invasive and harmful therapies that sought to change their behaviours or psychological makeup. Within the logics of Fordist-era capitalism, queerness and other breakings of traditional gender roles were threats to the need for the social reproduction of workers in heteronormative families. In this context, queer people were not just discriminated against and wrongly pathologised, but incarcerated and tortured merely for having romantic attraction or sexual relations.

By the early 1970s, however, many on the left as well as libertarian Szaszians had finally had enough of how queer people were represented and treated. Gay liberation activists were also angry and organised enough to do something about it. This culminated in gay liberation activists, backed by libertarian anti-psychiatry proponents and progressives alike, disrupting APA meetings to protest against the pathologisation of queerness.

Ultimately, this raised the question of why being gay had been pathologised in the first place, and it turned out to be far from clear why it should be. Eventually, the APA voted in 1973, almost unanimously, to demedicalise queerness. They realised that because being gay or lesbian did not cause suffering or disability, there was no clear reason to list it as a medical pathology. Yet while this was an important move in gay liberation, it did not improve the image of psychiatry in the eyes of its critics. As Richard McNally has observed, 'the democratic process by which the APA resolved the controversy' was taken, rightly or wrongly, to show 'that psychiatry had no principled basis for distinguishing mental disorders from other aspects of human functioning'.[4]

It was this, in large part, that finally brought American psychiatry into full crisis, and forced it to confront and, to an extent, incorporate the Szaszian critique. To do this, psychiatrists turned back to, and rapidly expanded, Kraepelin's more biocentric approach, which was largely consistent with Szasz's affirmation of the objectivity of the concept of the 'normal' brain. While psychiatrists such as Samuel Guze had been arguing for a neo-Kraepelinian approach since the 1950s, the key psychiatrist to instigate the shift was Robert Spitzer. It was Spitzer that led the taskforce for the third edition of the DSM, which would go on to become a surprise best-seller and usher in a new age of psychiatric power.

ROBERT SPITZER AND THE DSM-III

Spitzer – born in New York in 1932 and educated at the New York University of Medicine – viewed the DSM revision process as a golden opportunity. While the previous editions did not even contain a definition of mental illness and were barely used by clinicians, Spitzer would seek to provide a firm concept of mental disorder that would allow robust scientific research to guide future practice. He would also get rid of the psychoanalytic influence, tighten up diagnostic criteria for each diagnosis to avoid misdiagnosis, and provide a firmly medical conception of mental disorder. It was this that would allow the DSM to go from a relatively minor book, not taken seriously by most clinicians, to among the most influential books in the modern world. It would not just be an international best-seller – generating huge income for the American

Psychiatric Association with each new edition – but come to be used by researchers, insurance companies, and government policy makers alongside clinicians.

To understand Spitzer's work, recall here that Szasz had argued that psychoanalytic conceptions of illness were pseudo-scientific, and that real illness reflected abnormality of biological structure or functioning. Starting their work in 1974 against the backdrop of this critique, Spitzer's team largely dropped the reliance on psychoanalytic theory – at least implicitly conceding to Szasz that the Freudian approach lacked evidence – and instead tried to develop purely descriptive criteria with necessary and sufficient conditions for each diagnosis. This sought to help make diagnosis reliable, with greater utility for research, and it led to expanding the number of diagnostic classifications, which were grouped into different kinds of disorders, such as developmental disorders, anxiety disorders, and so on.

The most fundamental addition, though, was the newly clarified concept of 'mental disorder', which was based on the notion of individual 'dysfunction'. This new conception required there to be either biological, psychological, or behavioural dysfunction as a necessary condition for counting an ailment as a genuine disorder. The hope was to bring psychiatry more in line not just with somatic medicine and the biological and cognitive sciences – and their Darwinian notions of functioning – but also with the rising behaviourist science of biological organisms.

In making this shift, Spitzer, at least implicitly, conceded to the Szaszian view that underlying dysfunction was necessary for disorder. However, he rejected Szasz's overly rigid Cartesian binary between the psychological and the neurological, allowing that the dysfunction could be at either level, or even detected in behaviours taken to express underlying dysfunction. The term 'disorder' was thus adopted rather than 'disease' since the former leaves open whether the dysfunction is at the biological or merely psychological levels, while 'disease' is generally associated with biology only. If someone was shown to be, say, statistically subnormal on cognitive tests, or was consistently maladaptive in their behaviour, this could be sufficient, on the Spitzerian account, for considering there to be a mental disorder. And this was so even if a biological basis had not been verified.

Alongside the dysfunction criteria, Spitzer also realised that most of the mental disorders in previous editions were associated with harm as well as dysfunction. For that matter, this was true of somatic illnesses too. Importantly, Spitzer himself thought that queerness may be dysfunctional from an abstract Darwinian perspective, but even if so, it was nonetheless benign, making it different from genuine illnesses. Given this, Spitzer's team decided to include the criteria that a condition must also be harmful to be considered a mental disorder, where 'harm' is conceptualised in terms of either distress or disability. Thus, the definition the DSM-III provided was, in its final form, as follows:

> each of the mental disorders is conceptualized as a clinically sig-
> nificant behavioral or psychological syndrome or pattern that
> occurs in an individual and that is typically associated with either
> a painful symptom (distress) or impairment in one or more
> important areas of functioning (disability). In addition, there is
> an inference that there is a behavioral, psychological, or biological
> dysfunction, and that the disturbance is not only in the relation-
> ship between the individual and society.[5]

By making both harm and individual dysfunction necessary, and jointly sufficient, for ascribing mental disorder, it was hoped that the concept would be inherently defended against wrongfully pathologising social deviance or benign dysfunction – and would bring psychiatry, its research programmes, and practices, in line with the theories and practices of general medicine and frameworks for understanding cognitive disablement.

And yet, rather than being a new conception of mental disorder, what this signalled was a return to Galton's paradigm. Just as Galton had thought about all mental disability, mental disorders were to become individual Darwinian dysfunctions in cognition or neurology, understood in relation to 'normal' functioning, and often taken to stem from hereditary dispositions that can be triggered in specific contexts. In pontificating over how to define dysfunction, Spitzer precisely associated it with lower productivity in relation to the statistical norm. In his own words, the concept of

> *inherent disadvantage*, relative to other individuals, that results from not being able to function in that area is useful. For example, an individual who is not able to test reality because of delusions or hallucinations, or an individual who is not able to function occupationally because of depression, is at a clear inherent disadvantage in efforts to satisfy basic biological and psychological needs.[6]

In line with such discussions, a mass new research programme arose among philosophers of science, who sought to clarify the precise nature of biostatistical dysfunction with ever greater precision. By 1975, for instance, in what would come to be among the most influential accounts of the nature of health in the late twentieth century, the philosopher Christopher Boorse had argued that dysfunction was an objective concept that referred only to statistically subnormal functioning when compared to all members of the same species, sex, and age.[7] In turn, the dysfunctions that emerged through such theoretical analyses would be reified by Galtonian paradigm research, which focused on finding individual cognitive and biological deficits as compared to a neurotypical norm, albeit this time supplemented with elements of the behaviourist tradition and technology far more advanced than that which had been available in Galton's time.

Importantly too, while there was some resistance to this pathologisation, the Szaszian anti-psychiatry analysis was not just increasingly irrelevant. If anything, it had been part of the very process that allowed the Galtonian approach to return stronger than ever. By relying on and reinforcing the idea that pathology is a matter of structural or functional 'abnormality', and seeing this as a simple, objective matter, Szasz and his followers fully bought into the logics of the pathology paradigm. Instead of building a new approach, they had just tried to limit the reach of the dominant paradigm from within by suggesting that mental illnesses needed to be verified as having a biological element to be deemed real maladies.

Looked at this way Darwinian rather than Freudian conceptions of neurological abnormality were thus perfectly legitimate. All psychiatry needed to do was turn away from Freud's equilibrium conception of health and towards a medicalised conception of normal functioning and begin researching again at the genetic and neurological levels. And so it was that anti-psychiatry helped open the door for Galtonian psychiatry and ideology to not just return but become fully hegemonic.

THE LIMITS OF BIOLOGICAL PSYCHIATRY

The decade following the release of the DSM-III had seen both a mass expansion of psychiatry and a turn from Freudian models to biocentric and cognitivist approaches to mental health. This meant that mental disorder came to be seen as stemming from a 'broken brain' or glitchy mind, and should be fixed primarily by biomedical, cognitive, or behavioural intervention. We see this shift exemplified, for instance, in the neuroscientist Nancy Andreasen's 1984 book *The Broken Brain: The Biological Revolution in Psychiatry*. Andreasen positioned Kraepelin rather than Freud as the father of modern psychiatry, and was confident enough to state that psychiatric disorders were now medical conditions 'in the same sense that cancer or high blood pressure are'.[8]

While this shift was led by enthusiastic neuroscientists and psychiatrists, it was embraced much more widely, and by 1990 it made sense for President Bush to declare the next ten years the 'Decade of the Brain'. Bush's support was also – so it was thought – supposed to be economically prudential. The hope was that, rather than expensive personal therapy or societal changes, new drugs could be developed and then mass produced to ease the suffering of psychiatric patients cheaply and efficiently. Following this, the 1990s, and then the 2000s, brought a huge increase in funding for the National Institute of Mental Health in the United States, and similar organisations elsewhere. New mental and neurological disorders were recognised, classified, and diagnosed in ever greater numbers. And new psychiatric therapies and drugs were developed and implemented to treat them.

In turn American psychiatry was increasingly exported around the world. In the place of the old European empires and their colonial asylums, the new psychiatric imperialism mainly came in the guise of ideas, diagnoses, and medications. As the work of Ethan Watters[9] has shown, it was primarily drug companies that drove the exportation of Western diagnoses as and where the opportunity arose. This led to the erasure of local understandings in favour of biomedical narratives that were useful for American and European pharmaceutical companies to profit. While the suffering was of course real, the cultural expansion of biomedical narratives primarily followed the logic of the markets. According to these companies, these new biomedical treatments would help those experiencing mental distress or illness in ways that would far surpass those based on more local understandings.

And yet despite all of this, mental health did not improve. On some estimates, our collective mental health has flatlined since the 1980s, while on others, it may even have gotten worse. When it comes to the United States, this has been discussed by Robert Whitaker, a journalist and influential critic of biomedical psychiatry. As he noted in 2010: 'In 2007 the disability rate (for mental illness) was 1 in every 76 Americans. That's more than double the rate in 1987, and six times the rate in 1955'.[10] This was despite a mass rise in the use of both new and old psychotropic medications. Indeed, these increased year on year until they were prescribed to almost a quarter of the UK population in 2018[11] and around 16.5% of the US population[12] in 2020. While it should again be acknowledged that these did and do genuinely help some people – and even save many lives – for many they did not help, or not enough. And for others still, they made things worse.

The mass failure of this project can most starkly be seen in the words of Thomas Insel, who had led the National Institute of Mental

Health between 2002 and 2015. It was in 2017 that he finally made the startling admission that:

> I spent 13 years at NIMH really pushing on the neuroscience and genetics of mental disorders, and when I look back on that I realize that while I think I succeeded at getting lots of really cool papers published by cool scientists at fairly large costs – I think $20 billion – I don't think we moved the needle in reducing suicide, reducing hospitalizations, improving recovery for the tens of millions of people who have mental illness.[13]

A range of studies show that psychiatric medications, on average, tend to have at least a small positive impact despite their limited utility and risk of harmful side effects.[14] So if everything else had stayed the same mental health should have improved given the increased use of medications. It may therefore be that to understand what went wrong, we must again turn to the broader social, economic, and technological changes that began around the same time Spitzer's team was readying the DSM-III for publication.

8

Post-Fordism as a mass
disabling event

In the summer of 1975, a speaker at the Conservative Research Department in Great Britain was giving a talk on how the British Conservative Party should avoid the extremes of left and right. Instead, he was arguing, they should forge a new 'middle way'. Suddenly, he was interrupted by a woman who stood up and pulled a book from her briefcase. Brandishing the book so all could see it, she stated 'This is what we believe', before banging the book down on the table. The woman who had interrupted the speech was none other than the newly elected leader of the Conservative Party, Margaret Thatcher. And the book she had declared her allegiance to was titled *The Constitution of Liberty*, written by Thomas Szasz's idol, the economist Friedrich Hayek.

Four years later, in 1979, Thatcher was elected to be Prime Minister, and began ushering in Hayekian policies to the United Kingdom. Around the same time, Ronald Reagan in the United States also began implementing Hayekian policies. It is to this shift that we now turn. For the shift from Keynesian economics to Hayekian economics is vital for understanding the rising tide of mental health problems and the inability of biological psychiatry to effectively fight it.

The basic idea of neoliberalism, as summarised by David Harvey, was that 'human well-being can best be advanced by liberating individual entrepreneurial freedoms and skills within an institutional framework characterized by strong private property rights, free markets, and free trade'.[1] In practice this meant privatisation, deregulation, and austerity. Following the culture wars and economic recession of the 1970s, Thatcher and Reagan essentially sought to reverse the welfare capitalism of the earlier twentieth century. While Chile, guided by US pressure, had experimented with neoliberal policies several years earlier, it was during the early 1980s that Britain and the United States each began massively rolling back the state and diminishing the welfare system.

In the wake of changes made by Thatcher and Reagan, neoliberalism was quickly enforced across much of the rest of the world. It was globalised through international financial institutions such as the World Trade Organization and International Monetary Fund, and through US imperial pressure. As state communism fell, even Russia and China increasingly liberalised their economies to fit in – to at least some extent, and with mixed success – with the new global system. From around the same time, traditionally left-leaning political parties in liberal democracies, such as the British Labour Party and the Democratic Party in the United States, also shifted to the right. This was largely as organised labour was crushed by neoliberal governments and neoliberal ideology was propagated by the press. In this context, aspirational voters were choosing the ideal of individual freedom offered by neoliberalism over the progressive ideals, and higher taxes, of more collectivist politics.

This was to have profound effects on pretty much every aspect of human life. Indeed, as Harvey writes, neoliberal ideology had since 'become hegemonic as a mode of discourse'. It has, he goes on, 'pervasive effects on ways of thought to the point where it has become incorporated into the common-sense way many of us interpret, live in, and understand the world'.[2] As we will see below, our experiences and understandings of mental health were far from immune to this more general shift.

The end of the Soviet Union, and other actually existing attempts to build communism, also brought the rise of what the social theorist Mark Fisher retrospectively called 'capitalist realism'. This was his term for what he described as a 'pervasive atmosphere, conditioning not only the production of culture but also the regulation of work and education, and acting as a kind of invisible barrier constraining thought and action' that made capitalism seem like the natural and only possible way of organising the world. Within this context, class consciousness and thus the idea that capitalism could be meaningfully challenged or replaced was stifled. The harms of capitalism were recognised, but even then the possibility of imagining and fighting for a coherent alternative became less possible. All that was left was to strive for normality and wealth, in competition with all the other unwell workers.

For Thatcher, poverty itself was seen not as a structural problem but as an individual one. People are in poverty, she stated in a 1978 interview, because they 'don't know how to budget, don't know how to spend their earnings'. Ultimately, for her this came down to them having an individual 'personality defect'[3] In a later speech, she posited that 'poverty is not material but behavioural'.[4]

These shifts are relevant for understanding the worsening of mental health partly in connection with rising inequality. Over this period, the unfettered market allowed the rich to get richer, leading to a further accumulation of capital in the hands of a few. At the same time, workers' rights were weakened, workers had less control over their workplaces, and they also had to work longer hours than ever before. The mental health effects of this have been detailed by Iain Ferguson in his 2017 book *Politics of the Mind: Marxism and Mental Distress*. Ferguson draws on Marx's concept of alienation to argue that changes in the workplace have led to worsening mental health outcomes. On the one hand, he writes

the mental health of those in employment has [...] suffered as a result of the neoliberal policies of the past three decades. In 2015/2016 stress accounted for 37 percent of all work-related absences and 45 percent of all working days lost due to ill-health. The intensification of work, which has been a key element of the neoliberal project, is one reason for this epidemic of work-related stress.[5]

On the other hand, those in low-paid employment or unemployment experience the worst effects. For instance, one 2017 UK report Ferguson cites found mental health problems were directly linked to income and unemployment: 73 per cent of people in the lowest household income bracket experienced mental health problems in their lifetime, while 59 per cent of those in the highest bracket did. In turn, a 'substantial majority of those currently unemployed (85 percent) report that they have experienced a mental health problem compared to 66 percent in paid employment'.[6] Indeed, Ferguson further notes, austerity measures have also been associated with a huge rise in suicides. For instance, when neoliberal austerity was enforced in Greece, suicide rates shot up in line with rising levels of unemployment.

At the same time, community care for people experiencing mental illness did not improve, and many neoliberal governments cut funding for health services. Hence in a myriad of ways the neoliberal era seems to have worsened mental health. And the biomedical approach, by only treating symptoms with blunt biomedical tools, was unable to stem the rising tide of mental illness and disablement.

THE NEW ALIENATION

One way to help make sense of worsening mental health outcomes during this period is to update Marx's notion of alienation to fit the current era. As has been noted already, alienation refers to an estrangement from self and others that increased within the conditions of labour under capitalism. For Marx, the structural arrangements of capitalism mean that workers are deprived of control of the means of production and are instead defined by their instrumental value to generate profit. Marx argued that when workers are effectively forced to sell their labour just so others could profit it is harmful to the worker, stunting both their health and growth. Moreover, less worker control meant greater estrangement from their creative activity and the products of work:

the spontaneous activity of the human imagination, of the human brain and the human heart, operates on the individual independently of him – that is, operates as an alien, divine or diabolical activity – so is the worker's activity not his spontaneous activity. It belongs to another; it is the loss of his self.[7]

Importantly, while Marx did not use the language of mental health, the effects he indicates are precisely what would today be described in medical terminology. In being alienated, he writes, the worker 'denies himself, does not feel content but unhappy, does not develop freely his physical and mental energy but mortifies his body and ruins his mind'.

It is important to stress, however, that Marx was writing during a time when workers' alienation arose mainly in factories where material products were manufactured. To understand alienation today in post-industrial economies, several other changes accompanying the rise of neoliberalism need to be considered. The first is the mass rise of reliance on emotional labour. This regards what the sociologist C. Wright Mills termed the 'personality market', whereby 'personal or even intimate traits of employees are drawn into the sphere of exchange, become commodities in the labor market'. While this has always been the case to some extent, it has become much more central in economic relations following the shift from manufacturing economies to service economies. In a modern services economy, ways of feeling and relating, for instance in kindliness and friendliness, 'become aspects of personalized service or of public relations of big firms, rationalized to further the sale of something'.[8]

While Mills documented this in the 1950s, the mental health effects of emotional labour were first properly comprehended three decades later by the US sociologist Arlie Russell Hochschild. By this time services dominated the US economy, bringing new forms of mass alienation Hochschild detailed in her 1983 book *The Managed Heart: Commercialization of Human Feeling*. Hochschild illustrated this with the example of a flight attendant:

For the flight attendant, the smiles are a *part of her work*, a part that requires her to coordinate self and feeling so that the work seems to be effortless. To show that the enjoyment takes effort is to do the job poorly. Similarly, part of the job is to disguise fatigue and irritation, for otherwise the labor would show in an unseemly way, and the product – passenger contentment – would be damaged. Because it is easier to disguise fatigue and irritation if they can be banished altogether, at least for brief periods, this feat calls for emotional labor.[9]

In Hochschild's account, this incurs massive emotional costs, whereby 'the worker can become estranged or alienated from an aspect of self'.[10] As workers she interviewed revealed, a key outcome of this is stress and situational depression.[11] Hence already by the time she was writing in the early 1980s, telephone companies were giving their workers free drugs such as Valium or codeine in order to help them bear the costs of emotional labour to more easily allow more efficient production.[12] At the same time, pharmaceuticals were increasingly prescribed year after year, in many cases to people working long hours in the new services industries. And this has only increased in the decades following Hochschild's initial analysis.

Cognitive labour is equally important to consider alongside the services economy and rising reliance on emotion labour. Around the same period, new technological innovations, most notably, the personal computer, the internet, and the digital revolution more broadly, led to the rise of what has been termed post-Fordism or 'cognitive capitalism'. Traditional industrial capitalism was based on 'the accumulation of physical labour' and material production, but since around 1975, 'the object of accumulation consists mainly of knowledge, which becomes the basic source of value, as well as the principal location of the process of valorisation'.[13]

The cognitive alienation of this era and how it harms mental health has been examined by Franco 'Bifo' Berardi in his penetrating 2009 book *The Soul at Work: From alienation to autonomy*. As Berardi notes, architects, travel agents, solicitors, computer programmers, and so forth all use relatively similar machines – mostly computers, mobile phones, etc. – but have different specialist knowledges with specific cognitive contents that produce surplus value. Because of this, much capital is currently created by countless solitary individuals, sitting in front of screens, typing, scrolling, calculating, and using different cognitive contents to produce an endless variety of cognitive contents from which capital can be mined.

Within this phase of capitalism, Berardi documents the rise of a form of societal organisation he calls the 'factory of unhappiness'. In the Fordist era, jobs had tended to be stable, and to require being one small part of a manufacturing process that could be left behind at the end of the day. The worker would then return to their private life where they could relax or pursue their personal interests. By contrast, in the post-Fordist era, distinctions between home and work, public and private, employed and unemployed collapsed as work became casualised and precarious while workers became always reachable through phones and emails.

At the same time, our relationship with capital and production has increasingly spread beyond work, and into the weekend and evening, in other ways. Browsing online means being constantly bombarded with advertisements; posting on social media creates content that is then turned into profit by the owner of the site; and use of an app may be granted only after filling in a brief survey. Any moment we are online or using an ever-growing host of apps, we are constantly yet subtly guided by algorithms designed to direct our attention, document our behaviours, stoke our emotions, and influence our desires in the service of capital.

The result of these combined factors, in Berardi's words, has been that mental health deteriorates as our 'desiring energy is trapped in the trick of self-enterprise, our libidinal investments are regulated according to economic rules, our attention is captured in the precariousness of virtual networks: every fragment of mental activity must be transformed into capital'.[14] Thus for Berardi, post-Fordism brings a new form of alienation 'marked by the submission of the soul, in which animated, creative, linguistic, emotional corporeality is subsumed and incorporated by the production of value'.[15] According to his analysis, this kind of instability and fluidity contributes to constant depression, anxiety, and panic – all problems that became increasingly prevalent towards the end of the twentieth century, and skyrocketed in post-Fordist economies following the turn of the millennium.

NEURODIVERGENT DISABLEMENT

If boredom was distinctive of the work of the monotonous Fordist era, anxiety and depression are distinctive of post-Fordism. But this was not the only effect of these shifts in capitalism. Just as the Industrial Revolution brought new bodily norms, so too did the digital revolution and cognitive capitalism bring newly restrictive cognitive, emotional, and attentive norms in both the classroom and the workplace. The sensory-cognitive intensification of capitalism meant that a great many more people were either shut out of education or work, at least to varying extents, and were thus harmed in a different way. Rather than being positioned as 'ordinary' workers with mental health problems, they were disabled, and pushed towards the surplus population, even if some did manage to work despite this. In this context, new disability diagnoses initially referred to as 'shadow syndromes' – milder versions of existing diagnoses – also began being increasingly applied during childhood as well as to adults. More people were harmed by, and considered unsuited to, the needs and organisation of the new economy and its sensory, cognitive, and emotional requirements.

One key example is definitive of our age: autism. When it comes to the requirement for sociality, hyper-flexibility, and emotional labour, it is not just that stress levels have risen among the general population. It is also that the autism diagnosis, which had previously been restricted to a relatively limited number of cases, was radically expanded.[16] The broadening of autism into a spectrum was first tentatively suggested in 1979, the year Thatcher became Prime Minister, and began to expand over the following decade. Since the 1990s and 2000s especially, the spectrum has continually widened as an ever-rising percentage of the population fall short of the social, communicative, and sensory processing capabilities required by the new economy. The expansion of the autism diagnosis has been directly applied to people who are blocked from working in the services economies of the post-Fordist era. Hence, for instance, in 2021, a UK government report found that only 22 per cent of the autistic population were in employment despite many desiring to work.[17]

Highly relevant here is not just the emotional requirements of the services economy but the invasive sensory and information environments of the modern world, where economic relations require a constant bombardment of lights, advertising, screens, and so forth. In this context, high levels of anxiety in the autistic population have been associated in a variety of studies with what is framed as 'sensory over-responsivity'.[18] As one autistic person writes:

I struggle with bright lights and noise, I hate swaying or spinning motion, I cannot cope in big crowds where there are a lot of competing noises, and my sense of smell is often overpowering [...] It feels like my brain is being squeezed and all of my muscles tense up. My heart races fast and my breathing quickens. At this point, I lose the ability to think straight and my thoughts sound like they are overlapping and nonsensical.[19]

Simultaneously, neoliberalism and cognitive capitalism have also brought a pace in the tempo of life that has increasingly disabled those whose cognitive processing fits a less hurried pace. As Robert Hassan writes, the Fordist era and 'machine and factory based process had a specific tempo, and it was much slower than it is today'. By contrast, he goes on, today:

To be efficient is [...] to be physically, cognitively, psychologically and metaphorically able to 'move fast' when the time comes. This may be a flexibility to change your job often, a flexibility regarding the way one does a job, a flexibility in your opinions (dogmatism is out for most of us), a flexibility with respect of your physical location, or [... to] be able to 'synchronize' with fast-changing scenarios and rapidly unfolding events.[20]

These economic requirements do not just affect adults in work, but also children, whose environments will be similarly determined by the broader social conditions of the time. With all this in mind, it is unsurprising that a diagnosis where a central criterion is 'resistance to change' or 'need for sameness' would rapidly expand from 1980 onward. Never before have humans been required to live at the velocities necessitated by the shifting and precarious post-Fordist world.

We also see similar dynamics with other diagnoses. Consider here how over this period attention too became increasingly scarce given the constant sensory and informational bombardments of the post-Fordist era. For instance, as Berardi stresses, in contemporary society we find

> visual and auditory messages in every inch of our visual space and every second of our time, The diffusion of screens in public spaces (railway stations, airports, city streets and squares), is an integral part of this abusive occupation [...] Everywhere, attention is under siege [...] A cognitive space overloaded with nervous incentives to act; this is the alienation of our times.[21]

As the norms of cognitive attention became increasingly restrictive there came a great rise in people disenabled in such a way that came to be diagnosed as Attention Deficit Hyperactivity Disorder (ADHD). In line with Berardi's example, research shows that more general sensory processing issues are common among children with ADHD and is associated with anxiety, interpersonal problems, and problems in educational attainment.[22] Since the 1980s children and adults diagnosed with ADHD have, ever increasingly, required medication to enable functioning in line with educational and workplace demands alongside the cognitive stresses of day-to-day life. For instance, one study found that between 1992 and 2013 the prevalence of children under 16 taking medications for ADHD increased between three- and four-fold.[23] Yet despite many finding medications useful, it remains the case that employees with ADHD tend to have chronic employment issues and are 60 per cent more likely to be fired when compared with the general population.[24] Indeed, many of the questions on standard ADHD screening tests relate directly to work skills, including questions about trouble focusing on repetitive work or with planning and organising.

This is not to say these problems did not exist prior to post-Fordism, or that things like autism or ADHD are not real disabilities. They are no less 'real' than diabetes or dementia. But existing forms of difficulty or disablement, while to some extent grounded in atypical neurological development, were in many cases hugely amplified in this phase of capitalism. Traits that were previously relatively benign became associated with some level of disablement, while traits that might have only been minimally disabling became significantly so. This has increased as the intensification of capitalism has become so pervasive: it structures or at least taints almost every aspect of sensory experience and cognitive processing in day-to-day life, whether in work or in leisure time. It is not the technology itself that is the problem but rather that technology is primarily used in service of capital, and the various systems of domination that capitalism is intertwined with, which leave so many of us constantly fatigued, far beyond the workplace. And this increasingly stifles the development and thriving of even those who diverge in a relatively minimal way from the ever-more restrictive cognitive norms of the age.

Indeed, these forms of disablement are in significant part an extreme expression of issues faced across the general neurological spectrum of humanity. After all, the same problems affect everyone, not just those who are disabled in these conditions. In the scientific literature more generally, for instance, modern artificial lighting has been associated with depression and other health conditions;[25] excessive exposure to screentime has been associated with chronic overstimulation, mental health conditions, and cognitive disablement;[26] and noise annoyance has been associated with a two-fold increase in depression and anxiety, especially relating to noise pollution from aircraft, traffic, and industrial work.[27] One study based on parental reports found that 5.3 per cent of playschool children now experience clinically significant levels of sensory processing disablement.[28] And we have already seen how the alienation that follows intensive cognitive or emotional labour is harmful to all.

Yet instead of being understood as relationally constituted between individual and environment, through the neo-Galtonian pathology paradigm these forms of disablement were framed as individual deficit. Interestingly, as Goldstein observed in 2012, most psychometricians 'still appear to be working within the parameters set out around the time of Galton; typically either developing more complex modelling and analysis procedures or devising new measuring instruments'.[29] When it comes to disability or disorder classification, as the psychologist Kurt Danzinger has detailed, this followed an older tradition whereby

the Galtonian use of statistics greatly facilitated the artificial creation of new groups whose defining characteristic was based on performance on some psychological instrument, most commonly an intelligence test. A score on a mental test conferred membership in an abstract collectivity created for the purposes of psychological research. This opened up untold vistas for such research because psychologists could create these kinds of collectivity ad infinitum and then explore the statistical relationships between them.[30]

Simultaneously, in line with Kraepelin's 1919 proposal of a 'mass psychiatry' that would test ability for everything including the capacity to work, by the end of the twentieth century, psychometric testing had rapidly expanded. By this time, a dizzying array of new tests were developed and implemented in educational and workplace settings, for instance, to test employability or competence for even relatively menial roles.[31]

In psychiatry, these new classifications were often reified through the notion of the 'latent variable', the assumed common cause inherent to the individual that underlay and could explain common results in psychometric testing. This allowed people with similar test results to be seen as sharing as-yet-unknown internal cognitive dysfunctions (empathy deficits, executive malfunctioning, etc.) or neurological dysfunctions (faulty mirror neurons, etc.). Biomedical researchers hypothesised that biomarkers would be found underlying these core cognitive deficiencies, leading to ever greater precision for diagnosis and treatment. The dominance of the pathology paradigm in this period allowed the idea to become wholly hegemonic that mental disorder stems from individual dysfunction.

NEOLIBERAL NORMALISATION

Cultural practices of normalisation, where the divergent are changed to become more normal, also shifted following the Spitzerian revolution and the rise of neoliberalism. One place we see this regards the prison complex. During this period the numbers of people with psychiatric disabilities and learning disabilities incarcerated in the prison system continued to grow. By the beginning of the twenty-first century over 50% of prison inmates in the United States and the United Kingdom had dyslexia, while around a quarter have ADHD. Moreover 'Some of the largest mental health centres in the United States currently operate behind bars, and 40 percent of people diagnosed with serious psychiatric disorders face arrest over their lifetimes'.[32] Today, people with mental disorder diagnoses, especially Black people, are among the most likely to be arrested, be harassed by the police, or die in police custody.

At the same time, a massively increased use of prison pharmaceuticals has been used alongside electronic tagging and biomedical risk assessment for prison inmates. Sociologist Ryan Hatch describes these as forms of 'technocorrections', which aim to reduce costs and subdue prison populations to make them more pliable. Thus by the year 2000 in the United States, for instance, '95 percent of maximum/high-security state prisons distributed psychotropics, compared to 88 percent of medium-security prisons and 62 percent of minimum/low-security prisons'.[33] Liat Ben-Moshe has also emphasised how conditions in prison tend to make mental health worse and that even talking therapy often serves oppressive functions in prisons. In one scenario she describes from a US prison:

Most of the participants in this group therapy scene are black, all are men and each of them is sitting in a cage. This is not a hyperbole description but mere fact. Each of the participants in this therapy session is in a small cage with bars and locks, including chains around their ankles (where would they escape to in their tiny cage, we are not told). The presumed therapist (who looks phenotypically white) is sitting outside the cages, asking the men who are lined up in a row of cages how they are doing, how they progressed this week, inquiring about new body injuries he can observe, and so on. A guard is constantly circling the cages.[34]

This, she notes, is the best mental health care inmates in US prisons tend to have access to.

Outside the prison system, normalisation has increasingly been taken to be obligatory from younger and younger ages as the notion of mental disorder came to be seen as hereditary harmful dysfunction. For instance, with autism, behavioural interventions still focus on using a reward system to normalise neurodivergence. This has grown into a multi-billion-dollar industry with huge schools established, especially across the United States, to help enforce normalisation. Despite the protests of countless autistic activists who argue that such efforts are themselves a harmful and dehumanising form of conversion therapy, behavioural therapies are thus still the most widely used response in the United Kingdom and the United States and are regularly touted as the 'gold standard' of autism interventions.

Through a similar logic, neoliberalism brought what Mark Fisher termed a 'privatization of stress'.[35] Here self-care became an ethical imperative for the individual, and a focus on self-management took over from state support, which was increasingly limited. Wellness and mindfulness industries have rapidly expanded in ways that function to help tired people adjust to increasingly long working hours and lower living conditions. In the United Kingdom, state support for anxiety or depression typically consists of a tiny number of CBT sessions, used with the explicit aim of returning people to work. This only increases alienation while leaving deeper problems and the social detriments of mental illness largely untouched. In some cases we also see a fusing of Szaszianism and neoliberal austerity politics. As Fisher drew attention to in 2009, in his discussion of the UK government benefits policy:

It is telling, in this context of rising rates of mental illness, that New Labour committed itself, early in its third term in government, to removing people from Incapacity Benefit, implying that many, if not most, claimants are malingerers.

In fact, he goes on,

A significant proportion of claimants, for instance, are people psychologically damaged as a consequence of the capitalist realist insistence that industries such as mining are no longer economically viable [...] Many have simply buckled under the terrifyingly unstable conditions of post-Fordism.[36]

Here we see how the culturally influential Szaszian notion that all 'mental illness' is really people pretending to be ill to avoid responsibility, combined with increased rates of stress, panic, and depression, feeds into neoliberal ideology. For Szasz as for the neoliberal, everyone is just an individual, fully responsible for their own positioning and their ability or inability to deal with it. Without a clearly defined and identifiable biological impairment, they are – following the influence of the Szaszian tradition and its grounding in a Hayekian worldview – considered malingerers, deemed to be pretending to suffer from false illnesses that do not really exist.

At the same time, in an echo of the 1940s, for those disabilities that were recognised, this period was accompanied by an increased framing of what were now seen to be brain disorders as economic 'burdens'. For instance, in a 2011 article, Gustavsson et al. wrote that:

The total cost of disorders of the brain [in Europe] was estimated at €798 billion in 2010. Direct costs constitute the majority of costs (37% direct healthcare costs and 23% direct non-medical costs) whereas the remaining 40% were indirect costs associated with patients' production losses [...] disorders of the brain likely constitute the number one economic challenge for European health care, now and in the future.[37]

In turn, the idea that mental disorders were brain disorders that stemmed from hereditary risk factors, coupled with the rise of neoliberalism and worries about 'production losses', brought new forms of reproductive control. Instead of being imposed by the state, however, they are either offered as services or left to private organisations. Where prenatal tests for neurodivergent disabilities are available, such as in the case of Down's syndrome, termination rates have rapidly increased, contributing to a decline in funding for social support and research into quality of life. In the United Kingdom, neurodivergent people have reported that private sperm banks regularly turn away donors due to diagnoses such as dyslexia or autism.[38] Given the neoliberal order, in such cases these processes are not determined by authoritarian government policy but by private organisations and market forces functioning in line with hegemonic neuronormative ideals.

By contrast, Anne McGuire has described how the child with closer proximity with neurotypicality is represented as a good investment:

The normative time of childhood – understood, simultaneously as a biological time of growth and development and as a sentimental/nostalgic time of innocence and hope – is precisely that time of seemingly infinite 'laters'; the child is positioned as 'early on' on the (normative) biological timeline and therefore is understood as having more of that desired and desirable commodity of time, more future yet-to-be-realized. In a neoliberal regime where 'time is money', the child is figured as 'time-rich' and so represents a good investment opportunity indeed.[39]

In short, the world was made increasingly uninhabitable for neurodivergent people, and then individuals or private companies were left to determine whether neurodivergent life should be reproduced in a world that fails to accommodate neurodivergence.

While each of these practices stems from a variety of different factors, part of what unites them is that each is in part predicated by Spitzer's idea that there is something not just inherently dysfunctional but also something inherently harmful about neurodivergent disabilities. Indeed, as I will come back to, this was sometimes to the point that it is considered better for some neurodivergent people to not exist at all. With this in mind, it is also important to consider that, during this time, the reach of the Galtonian paradigm grew further still. Around the turn of the millennium, conceptions of the good human life itself were also increasingly Galtonianised.

Culturally, we see this in how, through the neoliberal era a kind of individualism grew whereby the majority of people in the United States, according to a number of studies, came to identify as above-average in terms of intelligence.[40] Despite this being an illusion – by definition, it cannot be the case that most people are above-average – the idea that people's economic positioning and accumulation of material goods allowed this illusion to continue. Few wanted to be abnormal – weird, strange, and so forth. Yet in line with Galtonian ideology everyone wanted to be better than normal – and most believed themselves to be so.

Indeed, the Galtonianisation of the good life has occurred even among highly nuanced ethicists. For instance, in her 2006 book *Frontiers of Justice*, philosopher Martha Nussbaum proposed that the 'species norm (duly evaluated) tells us what the appropriate benchmark is for judging whether a given creature has decent opportunities for flourishing'. For Nussbaum, this makes normalisation a moral imperative, not just a medical one. Hence for autism, she proposes, special efforts' are required to help autistics 'attain the core capabilities that form part of that species norm'.[41] Such ways of thinking increasingly naturalised and individualised the harms associated with neurodivergence, and made the normative necessity of normalising neurodivergence likewise seem natural.

Around the same time, the demand to go to therapy continued to be enforced. The neoliberal privatisation of stress coupled with the ever-growing division of labour under capitalism brought an increased pressure for individuals to outsource their emotional processing to new and expanding therapy industries. Yet this has created a pressure for busy, cash-strapped workers to pay for unaffordable therapy that might not work and could even be harmful, while allowing wealthier people to position themselves as morally enlightened given their capacity to continually outsource their emotional processing to the best therapists, who can charge hundreds of pounds or dollars an hour that is then converted into cultural capital by wealthy clients.

More recently still physician-assisted suicide has been legalised, including in Canada, where it is increasingly used, as Jeremy Appel writes, 'for people with disabilities to apply to die rather than survive on meager benefits'.[42] As Appel details, while the rationale is about choice and harm reduction for people with terminal illnesses and in great pain, in practice 'euthanasia in Canada represents the cynical endgame of social provisioning within the brutal logic of late-stage capitalism'. It begins with starving 'you of the funding you need to live a dignified life', and then posits the decision to then die as a matter of freedom rather than coercion. While the choice for assisted suicide can genuinely increase autonomy, when this is granted in a broader neoliberal economy it leaves many little space for autonomy in practice.

Hence through neoliberal ideology, and eased by the Spitzerian conception of disorder as harmful dysfunction, normalisation, and eugenic control have continued. The main difference between contemporary approaches and Galton's is that, while Galton framed the social harmfulness of subnormal cognition more primarily at the societal level and thus a task for governmental intervention, contemporary approaches tend to frame the badness more primarily at the individual level and thus a matter of individual responsibility. On this privatisation of eugenic responsibility, no longer should neurodivergence be eliminated because it is a threat to society, but because it is inherently harmful and thus an inherent threat to its own bearer. Hence in her 2008 book *The Ethics of Autism*, bioethicist Professor Deborah Barnbaum argued that, once prenatal diagnostic technology is capable, there will be a moral obligation to abort autistic foetuses on the grounds that being autistic is inherently incompatible with living a good human life.

9

The neurodiversity movement

In June 1997 a young woman taking a part-time sociology degree read an article in the *New York Times*. Written by a journalist called Harvey Blume, the article, titled 'Autistics are Connecting in Cyber-space', instantly stoked Judy Singer's attention.[1] Given the recent wider availability of the internet, Blume wrote, 'many of the United States' autistics are doing the very thing the syndrome supposedly deters them from doing – communicating'. Indeed, it was not just that they found connecting easier online than in person. More than this, Blume detailed, an increasing number of these 'autistics are neither willing nor able to give up their own customs. Instead, they are proposing a new social compact, one emphasizing neurologi-cal pluralism'. That is, rather than giving in to pressure to act more 'normally', they were resisting this, and, in doing so, pushing back against the idea that autism itself was in need of fixing at all.

At that time, Singer was studying sociology at the University of Technology Sydney, in Australia. After previously dropping out of a medicine degree, Singer had turned to sociology to make sense of her political interests. One of these interests regarded the politics of disability. By the time that she read Blume's article, Singer had already begun to identify as being on the autism spectrum – then a little-known diagnosis, mainly associated with social and commu-nication problems alongside restricted interests and habits. Finding that many problems in her own life mirrored those of many autistic people, she had already joined various online autistic groups where she met other autistic people. What's more, Singer had also already begun thinking about autism through the sociological lens of disa-bility studies, which framed disablement as a societal more than an individual problem.

While all this made Blume's article pique her interest, what she related to most strongly was the 'neurological pluralism' that he described, and the related refusal to give up autistic customs in a neurotypical world. For more than anything else, Singer's own emerging understanding of autistic resistance was grounded in her experience of being part of the Jewish diaspora. That is, of being part of a group of outsiders who refused to assimilate – and who therefore paid the price.[2] After all, Singer herself was the daughter of a Holocaust survivor who had moved to Australia after the Second World War. And Singer herself had grown up feeling like an outsider even in the country of her birth. It was this heritage and experience, as part of a diaspora, that made her relate so strongly to this new politics of neurological pluralism and its associated refusal to give up autistic customs in the face of overwhelming societal pressure.

And so it was that on reading Blume's article, Singer quickly contacted him and signed up to become a member of this new community, based in a group called Independent Living on the Autism Spectrum. Within a year, she would not only immerse herself in this community, but go on to propose the more concise concept of 'neurodiversity' and provide the first sustained sociological analysis positioning these ideas in the field of disability studies. It was this that allowed her to call for a 'politics of neurological diversity, or neurodiversity' in a 1999 book chapter and thus, accompanied by Blume's reporting, help this pioneering community of autistic activists spark the rise of the neurodiversity movement across the globe.

In this seminal work, what Singer suggested was that neurodiversity should be recognised as 'an addition to the familiar political categories of class/gender/race'.[3] By conceptualising autism as an unrecognised intersection, Singer envisioned a new civil rights movement that could lead to the development of what she called an 'ecological' society. For Singer, this society would view neurodiversity much in the way conservationists view biodiversity, and would thus be geared towards changing social and material conditions to accommodate and conserve autistic ways of being. This would include making policy and practices more inclusive, and constructing cognitive niches to help cultivate autistic thriving and inclusion.

It would be precisely at odds with the dominant way of organising society, which segregated disabled people and routinely placed
great pressure on autistics to become more 'normal'. While the core
ideas of the movement were developed communally by countless
advocates and activists, Singer's contribution was to ground these
emerging ideas in the body of theory developed by disability studies.
It was this that established the theoretical basis that has since guided
the movement and its tactics and aspirations.

DISABILITY THEORY

To understand where these ideas first came from, we have to go back
a bit further. All the way back, in fact, to 1968, when a 30-year-old
Vic Finkelstein entered the United Kingdom as a refugee. Finkelstein was a political activist and had been imprisoned for his work
in the anti-apartheid movement. He was then banned from South
Africa for five years as he was suspected of being a communist.
What the authorities who imprisoned him didn't realise is that their
treatment of him would help him develop an idea that would change
the world.

For the authorities, the issue with Finkelstein was that, after
breaking his neck in an accident at 16, he had used a wheelchair ever
since. This meant that the government had been forced to make
adjustments to accommodate his impairment in order to imprison
him. But because they found ways to accommodate his impairment when it suited them, Finkelstein began to wonder whether
governments could – and, indeed, should – be pressured to make
accommodations by default. During his 18-month detention, he
also began to see more similarities between his experience of disability segregation and the apartheid he had been protesting. This led
him to explore how disability segregation was the result of contingent historical forces, which might possibly be changed.

These ideas were formalised in the 1970s by the Union of Phys-
ically Impaired Against Segregation, or UPIAS, a radical group of
Marxist disability activists who used to meet in a pub in London.
This group had been co-founded in 1972 by Finkelstein and another

disabled activist, Paul Hunt, who had been confined in institutions across England since he was a child. Based on their combined experiences, they came to see their disablement as the product of material social factors rather than a mere problem with the body. This way of thinking was clarified in a 1975 document titled *Fundamental Principles of Disability*, where they proposed what came to be called the 'social model' of disability.

They compared their new model to the individual or medical model. On the medical model, disability is taken to be caused by impairment or dysfunction. The idea is that something is wrong with a person's body, and that this causes that person to be unable to do normal things. On this traditional – and then still largely hegemonic – view, disability is a physiological tragedy that afflicts the individual. In many cases it is seen to inherently impede the possibility of living a full and good life. The best the individual can hope for is for medical treatment that minimises the disabling effects of their impairment in day-to-day life.

UPIAS rejected almost everything about this traditional framing. The core theoretical move made by UPIAS was to reject the causal link between bodily impairment and disablement. Instead, the Union of Physically Impaired Against Segregation proposed that it is

society which disables physically impaired people. Disability is something imposed on top of our impairments by the way we are unnecessarily isolated and excluded from full participation in society.[4]

In this view, material conditions and societal structures and practices, such as the lack of ramps to access buildings, 'imposed' disablement on people with physical impairment. This acknowledged that the impairment was real and part of the body but refused the assumption that this implied that disability is an individual tragedy. Viewed this way, the problem of disability is primarily one of marginalisation and oppression, not simply an individual medical matter. In other words, disability – or at least physical disability, since UPIAS excluded cognitive disability from their account – is no longer an individual medical problem but a problem relating to our social and material conditions.

While the social model is generally dated back to UPIAS, it is notable that other radical groups were developing similar insights at around the same time. For instance, as Sami Schalk has detailed, the Black Panthers, the US Black power and Marxist-Leninist organisation, had also begun seeing disabled liberation as bound up with collective liberation. Thus, by the late 1970s the Black Panthers were supporting radical disability activism. They 'took quickly to the social model of disability because it paralleled their own understanding of race and class oppression as stemming from the biases and failures of larger society'.[5]

The social model and other similar analyses developed elsewhere served as the theoretical basis for the disabled persons' movement, which mainly focused on physical disability for the first few decades. By focusing on how attitudes, physical structures, social expectations, and inadequate social support stifled the functioning and flourishing of disabled people, this movement was able to make significant gains in legal and social recognition, and in removing disabling barriers and challenging segregation. This broader movement is precisely why, today in the United Kingdom and other countries, construction routinely includes disabled car parking spaces, accessible toilets, ramps, and much more. This is because it brought about significant legal gains establishing disability rights in the United Kingdom, the United States, and elsewhere.

It was this way of thinking – rather than the Szaszian tradition – that early autistic activists drew on to begin challenging the idea that the disablement they experienced was wholly down to individual impairments. For instance, according to early autism rights advocate Jim Sinclair in a seminal 1993 article, the tragedy of autism occurred 'not because of what we are, but because of the things that happen to us' in a world that failed to accommodate autistic modes of processing and communication.[6] Autistic activists also argued that many problems in learning and understanding were down to sensory environments not accommodating autistic sensory processing styles. If physical structure, assumptions, expectations, and norms changed, much autistic disablement would be eased. They also argued that different minds could be seen as having different specialisations, and that divergent minds were not necessarily deficient.

It was this that led Blume to report on this emerging idea of 'neurological pluralism'. And as Singer has noted in retrospect, it also provided the 'intellectual framework' for her seminal work. Part of Singer's intervention was thus to formalise and clarify the insights of early autistic activists who applied the social model to neurological disability for the first time – and then used this as the basis for a new movement that would be part of the broader disabled persons movement.

DIVERSITY

The diversity in 'neurodiversity' comes from two sources. The first was the shift towards celebrating other forms of human diversity – cultural, sexual, and so forth – that arose following the major civil rights and pride movements of the twentieth century. Alongside these, early neurodiversity proponents began to ask whether neurological divergence could similarly be celebrated and be a locus of pride rather than being seen as an inherently tragic deviation. It was on this basis that neurodivergent people began to reclaim diagnostic classifications – autism, dyspraxia, and so forth – to allow recognition of shared forms of disablement while resisting the idea that this disablement stemmed from individual dysfunction. Notably, this allowed them to avoid the Szaszian mistake of denying recognition of disablement, while still positioning them to collectively push back against wrongful pathologisation and control. In this it kept the benefits of anti-psychiatry while avoiding its most harmful aspects.

The other source of the 'diversity' in 'neurodiversity', which is more relevant for understanding the most original contribution of neurodiversity theory, was the shift towards viewing biodiversity as a vital part of what sustains broader ecosystems. This had emerged in the 1960s as more scientists and activists became concerned with how capital's need to constantly consume natural resources for profit had not just led to the depletion of finite resources but the destruction of ecological equilibrium. By the 1990s the idea that biodiversity should be valued and conserved had entered the more progressive elements of public consciousness – and it was this that Singer and Blume extended to theorise the concept of neurological diversity.

We see this when we consider how the term 'neurodiversity' was first used in print by Harvey Blume in 1998. (While Blume helped develop the concept in email conversations with Singer, he was able to publish first.) Blume framed the concept precisely as a challenge to the concept of the normal brain. In his words:

The common assumption in cognitive studies these days is that [in] the human brain [...] the occasional bug is inevitable: hence autism and other departures from the neurological norm. [Autistics are suggesting] another way of looking at this. Neurodiversity may be every bit as crucial for the human race as biodiversity is for life in general. Who can say what form of wiring will prove best at any given moment?[7]

On Blume's understanding, the shift was from viewing mental functioning as either normal or abnormal – with the norm privileged as superior – to viewing different minds as having different cognitive specialisations within a broader cognitive ecosystem. For instance, 'computer culture', he wrote 'may favor a somewhat autistic cast of mind'. In stark contrast to the Galtonian tradition, the idea is that neurological diversity is vital for dealing with the complex problems that humanity will encounter in a constantly changing environment. From this view, then – even if we put aside ethical issues for a moment – it does not make sense to seek to eliminate neurodivergence, since this would impede our collective functioning.

It was this that "Singer's thesis brought together with insights from autistic activists and disability studies. In her thesis she grounded the idea of neurodiversity in critiques of the notion of the 'normal' body as well as the social model of disability. Although the constraints of the thesis didn't allow her to clarify the underlying theory in great detail, she suggested that the neurodiversity movement would work towards an 'ecological' society that would foster inclusion by constructing cognitive niches to accommodate autistic people. The more general idea was that for humanity to flourish, we need to both conserve diversity and to support divergence. Hence in stark contrast to the Galtonian tradition, which suggested the abnormal needed to be systematically pushed towards the norm, Singer sought to suggest that divergence itself was part of what constituted 'healthy' neurological functioning.

While Singer's work was seminal in helping formalise emerging autistic community theorising, it was also underdeveloped in a number of ways. There are at least two key issues worth drawing attention to here. One issue is that she limited her analysis to what she called 'high-functioning' autism. This left those autistic people who fall further from neuronormative standards back in an individualised medical model. In this, her analysis retained traces, to at least some extent, of the kind of ranking system definitive of the pathology paradigm. In turn, the practical implication of this is that her analysis would exclude many autistic (and otherwise neurodivergent) people who find a neurodiversity approach helpful and want to be included. Thus, her analysis did not go far enough, and if adopted may still end up reproducing rather than overcoming aspects of Galton's paradigm.

Second, it is also worth mentioning Singer's more recent response to criticisms of neurodiversity that suggest the approach is at odds with a scientific understanding that is promoted in mainstream psychiatry.[8] Singer's retort has been to simply claim that her concept was only ever supposed to be an 'activist' concept rather than a scientific one.

Her response is unsatisfactory for several reasons. First, Singer makes scientific claims that can generate testable hypotheses (such as that neurological diversity is vital for optimal functioning at the group level) while claiming that they are not scientific. This does not only seem contradictory. It also undersells the scientific and theoretical legitimacy of the neurodiversity perspective, risking making it seem as if it is closer to mere scientific sounding rhetoric rather than rigorous theory that has legitimate uses in scientific research.

Second, it has become clear since Singer developed her analysis that using the neurodiversity concept to change how we approach scientific research is not just possible but also vital for neurodivergent liberation. After all, as we have seen in earlier chapters, the way knowledge has been produced under Galton's paradigm is a big part of the problem, and hence changing how we approach the science of neurodiversity is vital. This can be seen when we consider the work of Nick Walker, and her proposal that neurodivergent liberation requires a paradigm shift. While neurodiversity theory has always been developed collectively, Walker is arguably one of the foundational neurodiversity theorists alongside Singer. Synthesising a second wave of neurodivergent community theorising, Walker clarifies the core differences between the pathology paradigm and the neurodiversity paradigm. It is thus to her work that we will now turn.

NEURODIVERSITY AS PARADIGM

It is striking that, like Singer, Walker is also a descendant of Jewish Holocaust survivors, who grew up in poverty as an undiagnosed autistic. And like Singer, Walker too would go on to make her seminal intervention not as a tenured academic but as an outsider student engaged in activist communities and online autistic groups. Unlike Singer, though, she honed her political views as a teenager involved in queer and anti-fascist activism on the American East Coast through the 1980s.

This was the time of the AIDS epidemic, when Ronald Reagan was presiding over the deaths of tens of thousands of people with AIDS while rolling back state welfare and ushering in the neoliberal era. Even though it followed the depathologisation of 'homosexuality', this period in some ways brought worsening discrimination against the queer community, who were wrongly scapegoated for the government's failure to deal with the crisis. And so it was this that, in line with her commitment to queer politics and her mistrust of the kind of binary thinking exemplified by the high-functioning/low-functioning distinction, Walker went on to propose an expanded analysis that surpassed Singer's work.

To understand this, it is helpful to skip forward to 2012. By that time, Walker was a mature graduate student at the California Institute for Integral Studies. She had also settled into a late autism diagnosis and had been engaged in online neurodiversity discourse for almost a decade. The movement and its theories had also expanded considerably, being adopted and developed by people with other diagnoses such as bipolar disorder as well as by people with so-called 'low-functioning' autism diagnoses, most notably the late autistic writer Mel Baggs. At the same time, new terms had begun to emerge, including 'neurodivergent' and 'neurominority', as additions to the concepts of 'neurotypicality' and 'neurodiversity'.

This all helped Walker to see that the neurodiversity concept was, in bits and pieces, and through collective effort, being expanded into a whole new 'paradigm'. Here Walker drew on a concept the philosopher and historian Thomas Kuhn[9] developed to help make sense of how sciences develop through history. A scientific paradigm, for Kuhn, is a set of assumptions and axioms that members of a scientific community share to ground their research for a given historical period. Kuhn showed that, in early historical stages scientific fields are pre-paradigmatic, but when they mature, they come to follow key prototypes and accompanying assumptions that later become adopted among the scientific community to ground their research. In turn, these paradigms can also sometimes change when the old paradigm becomes outdated and new prototypes and frameworks emerge, such as we see in the shift from Newton's paradigm to Einstein's paradigm.

Walker's conception of the neurodiversity 'paradigm' thus indicated the need for a new general set of fundamental assumptions, axioms, or principles that could form the basis for changing how we think about, study, and respond to human neurodiversity as such. This was first published in her seminal essay 'Throw away the master's tools: Liberating ourselves from the pathology paradigm', in an influential collection of autistic activist theorising titled *Loud Hands: Autistic People, Speaking*. It was here that Walker first argued that a new paradigm was beginning to emerge – and in turn that neurodivergent liberation would require the further development and implementation of this new paradigm.

Walker has summarised the core differences to the Galtonian pathology paradigm as follows. On the one hand:

The pathology paradigm starts from the assumption that significant divergences from dominant sociocultural norms of cognition and embodiment represent some form of deficit, defect, or pathology. In other words, the pathology paradigm divides the spectrum of human cognitive/embodied performance into 'normal' and 'other than normal', with 'normal' implicitly privileged as the superior and desirable state.

By contrast, she goes on,

The neurodiversity paradigm starts from the understanding that neurodiversity is an axis of human diversity, like ethnic diversity or diversity of gender and sexual orientation, and is subject to the same sorts of social dynamics as those other forms of diversity – including the dynamics of social power inequalities, privilege, and oppression. From this perspective, the pathologization of neurominorities can be recognized as simply another form of systemic oppression which functions similarly to the oppression of other types of minority groups.[10]

In short, for Walker, if we adopt this emerging understanding, instead of dividing groups into the normal and the pathological, we can instead frame them as having closer or further proximity to the neurotypical ideal. This raises the prospect of a more general shift in our scientific and cultural representations, analogous to the shift from viewing 'homosexuality' as a mental disorder to reframing it as a minority sexual orientation understood through queer theory. Hence, Walker writes, for neurodiversity proponents, the long-term aim should be understood as working towards a 'paradigm shift: a widespread supplanting of the pathology paradigm by the neurodiversity paradigm'.

It is my view that Walker's concept of the neurodiversity paradigm is important – and quickly caught on among neurodivergent activists – because it helps overcome the two key limitations of Singer's analysis. First, it allows us to recognise how neurodiversity has begun to form the basis for a different way of generating knowledge and thus justifying new approaches to policy and practice that would be based on this knowledge. Indeed, as Walker noted in 2021, in recent years it has precisely been the case that it is not only scientific research on neurodivergence (mainly autism so far) that has begun to change by incorporating social and ecological models of functioning. Research in literary studies, psychotherapy, musicology, and many other areas has also begun to emerge based on a neurodiversity paradigm framing. This framing helps show the significance of neurodiversity as a concept with applicability to scientific research, that can produce different knowledge to that which is generated by Galton's paradigm and hence help undo the latter's scientific as well as cultural hegemony.

The second key benefit of Walker's concept of the neurodiversity paradigm is that it allows us to formalise a broader analysis that goes far beyond autism. This has helped the framework become more inclusive, allowing people who find the paradigm helpful to adopt it regardless of what diagnosis they have. While some non-autistic people identified with the neurodiversity approach since more or less the beginning, this broader conception helped such identifications rapidly increase, expanding neurodiversity activism far beyond the autistic community.

NEURODIVERGENT MARXISM

That said, Walker only argued that the paradigm was beginning to emerge, and proposed that its consolidation should be seen as a goal for neurodiversity proponents to work towards. She didn't claim that it was fully formed and ready to be implemented. Neither did she explore in detail exactly what it would take to change the paradigm, framing the issue as one of changing how we think. As such, our current understanding of the proposed paradigm shift is limited.

The most fundamental limitation, which I have sought to address in this book, is that neither Walker nor any other neurodiversity theorist until now has provided a historical materialist analysis of the pathology paradigm. But here, by showing how the paradigm arose and caught on specifically because it allowed the individualisation and reification of neurodivergent disablement, we can better understand the significance and power of the pathology paradigm, as well as what it might take to overcome it. Since the pathology paradigm, and the way it naturalises increasingly restricted conceptions of normality, grew precisely to mirror the needs of the capitalist economy, it is these material conditions that need to be changed, not just our thinking. While changing our thinking is vital, we are unlikely to fully supplant the pathology paradigm while the capitalist global economic order remains dominant.

More generally, the key limitation of existing neurodiversity theory and activism is that it is more focused on changing our thinking and attitudes than on changing material conditions. To be clear, this is not to say that existing proponents ignore the material. Far from it. The embrace of the social model precisely demonstrates neurodiversity proponents' commitment to changing the social and material world when it comes to alleviating disablement. Still, this is usually limited to the individual, institutional, and, occasionally, legal levels rather than challenging the deeper structures of the economic order. Until now, there has been little to no analysis in neurodiversity theory and activism of political economy, or of whether liberation under capitalism is even possible. It is this that I think we need to go beyond. For as we have seen, the pathology paradigm – and its scientific quest to naturalise capitalist neuronormaitivity – was a product of those material conditions. While it has now become its own, distinct problem – and certainly could persist beyond capitalism – it seems unlikely to be supplanted without changing the deeper structures of society.

My historical analysis also allows us to see another more general problem with liberal approaches to neurodiversity theory. As we have seen, neurodiversity proponents argue that variations in mental functioning are like biodiversity, and that it takes more than just neurotypical minds for groups or even society as a whole to function. In an important sense this is a radical new idea that is the opposite of what Nazi ideology had held. The Nazi view, as we covered earlier, saw society as an organism that required uniformity of all its constituent parts. This meant that neurodivergent people had to be exterminated except to the extent they might prove useful for the economy at certain points. By contrast, neurodiversity holds that society requires diversity, and hence that divergence must be conserved. This places the demand on society to support neurodivergence rather than seeking to eliminate it.

Yet despite providing a stark difference to more fascistic ideologies of normality, some versions of neurodiversity theory can still be made to cohere with capitalist logics. For if the capitalists recognise that neurological diversity actually helps groups function, then capitalism can adopt a liberal neurodiversity perspective that conserves neurodivergent people as and to the extent that they are able to be mined for productivity. It will thus still have an in-group and an out-group, since this will inevitably only apply to some neurodivergent people – those with specific skills or who help group functioning – and not to others. Even while this is not, of course, something that would be endorsed by neurodiversity theorists, it is far from clear that the paradigm could truly be changed without simultaneously changing the deep structures of society. It is thus important to supplement existing neurodiversity theory with a more radical analysis.*

---

* Since I submitted this manuscript for publication, new archival evidence has come to light showing that the concept of neurodiversity as described by Singer and Blume was already in use in online autistic spaces in 1996. Moreover, this came to light following a string of statements from Singer on social media that have widely been regarded as transphobic. As such, while I think it is still worth engaging with her texts – which remain seminal studies of the movement – her role in formulating the theory will, over the coming years, need to be reassessed. I will address this in future publications.

10

Cognitive contradictions

Over the past decade the neurodiversity movement has grown at an incredible pace. The theories discussed in the previous chapter have formed the basis for neurodivergent praxis across much of the globe. This avalanche of activity occurred because it had to: because a sizeable portion of humanity could by this point no longer function within the increasingly strict neuronormativity imposed within the Empire of Normality. Neurodiversity activism has, over this time, been incorporated into everything from street protest to political lobbying; from unionism to research; and there has even been an attempt to include a commitment to ending neurodivergent oppression in a recently proposed draft constitution in Chile.

As a framework for praxis, neurodiversity theory is notable for not reproducing the old Cartesian dualism that has turned out to be, whether in its original or Szaszian form, so useful for capital and the state. Instead, the 'neuro' suffix emphasises the embodied nature of the mind, and that cognition is inseparable from the body, and beyond that, the world. This approach also avoids another key issue associated with the anti-psychiatry movement, which as we have seen legitimised a widespread denial of mental disability or illness. While neurodiversity proponents do challenge pathologisation in some cases, their challenge is directed more toward default pathologisation of those atypical minds considered to be unproductive, and not a blanket denial of mental illness as such. At the same time, in reclaiming disability rather than denying the fact of disability, neurodiversity proponents have been well-positioned to make demands of the state, as and where neurodivergent people find this useful.

A related reason this has provided a useful basis for praxis is that, as Steve Graby[1] notes, since it emphasises the embodied nature of cognition alongside the reality of disability, neurodiversity theory has helped connect mental health politics with the broader politics of disablement. This has helped with the development of a broader, more unified politics linked by neurodiversity theory and activism than is possible under a more Cartesian approach that seeks to strictly distinguish mental distress from bodily illness. Neurodiversity theory has thus helped provide a more unified politics that aims for collective liberation.

Finally, since neurodiversity theory centres disabled people as primary experts in their own experience, it provides a stark challenge to the authority of not just psychiatrists but also clinical psychologists, psychotherapists, and other clinical professions. This does not deny that members of these professions have some relevant expertise, but it both decentres that and uncovers the paradigm and ideology that has hitherto oriented, and often stifled, this expertise. Unlike the Szaszian tradition, which reproduces a medical model epistemology and thus remains led by clinical professionals, the neurodiversity movement challenges the authority of the physician and clinician class, instead orienting towards the needs of disabled and ill people more broadly.

Yet despite these improvements on previous attempts, neurodiversity theory and activism has remained, for the most part, within a liberal framework. The focus has been on a rights-based approach and on changing recognition, representations, and concepts. Neurodiversity advocacy has also tended to assume, at least implicitly, that neurodivergent liberation is possible under capitalism. This can be seen in so far as most neurodiversity activism has been geared towards attaining justice within capitalism rather than directly working towards a post-capitalist future.

At the same time, perhaps especially in the past five years, new neurodiversity industries have arisen, while existing industries have rapidly changed their branding to present themselves as neurodivergence-inclusive. What we are seeing is capitalism adapting to neurodivergence inclusion in so far as this can help capitalists profit. For instance, in the United Kingdom, airports now increasingly include sensory rooms, designed to make airports more accessible for children who are autistic or who have similar sensory processing disabilities, while supermarkets increasingly have 'autism-friendly' hours with reduced lighting. But we only see such changes in so far as they allow the consumer base to be increased. They do not lead to deep, systemic change.

We are also seeing the increased capture of neurodiversity advocacy by elites who are invested in maintaining the dominant system. For instance, the previous Conservative Member of Parliament and Health Secretary, Matt Hancock, has recently launched a neurodiversity charity that has made headlines in major UK papers. Despite this, Hancock and the government he served in have pursued austerity policies that are exceptionally harmful to neurodivergent people. His political commitments are inherently at odds with neurodivergent emancipation.

The rise of neuro-Thatcherism, whereby neurodiversity advocacy is turned into a business-oriented programme for unearthing neurodivergent strengths or 'super powers' and then mining those with these strengths may be useful for those neurodivergent people it helps into jobs. One possible by-product of this worth bearing in mind is that the more neurodivergent people who are recognised as vital for the workforce, the more potential power those people will have to organise as workers in unions. This could then have some utility for a politics of neurodiversity. Yet overall, neuro-Thatcherism does nothing to fundamentally challenge the deeper structures of society I have identified throughout this book as underpinning neurodivergent oppression. What's more, to the extent that neuro-Thatcherism becomes the dominant neurodiversity discourse, it will drown out the more radical and emancipatory modes developed by grassroots activists.

Of course, not all liberal activism coheres with the neuro-Thatcherist approach. There is a strong intersectional and more critical liberal component of the movement, especially at the grassroots level. One important development, among others, is the Disability Justice Movement in the United States. Proponents of this approach tend to demand rights while acknowledging that rights-based approaches tend to fall far short of justice, especially for multiply marginalised disabled people. Lydia X. Z. Brown and Shain M. Neumeier, for instance, have emphasised how disabled people at the margins are not protected by human rights laws. Moreover, they stress, even laws proposed to protect disabled people can end up being used to harm them, as in the case of guardianships and involuntary commitment.[2]

In line with a disability justice approach, one of the more positive recent developments is the theory and praxis of neuroqueering. Stemming from the work of Nick Walker and Remi Yergeau, neuroqueering focuses on embracing weird potentials within one's neurocognitive space, and turning everyday comportment and behaviour into forms of resistance.[3] This has provided a new tool for combatting neuronormativity from within the constraints imposed by history and current material conditions. By queering the social world, new possibilities are carved out for the future, helping us not just challenge aspects of the current order but to start collectively imagining what a different world could be like.

Unlike some 'class-first' Marxists, I think these more intersectional approaches are extremely important, and provide a helpful contrast to neuro-Thatcherism. If neuronormative ideology enforces a pervasive fog, restricting our thought, agency, and action, neuroqueering prods this, helping identify its weak points. And disability justice approaches help build vital community resources and projects outside of state-sanctioned interventions. Such efforts not only change local material conditions but also allow an expansion of neurodivergent consciousness and agency at individual and collective levels. Still, even these approaches tend to avoid deeper analysis of neurodivergent oppression in relation to the political economy. Given what I have sought to show in this book, it seems worth clarifying exactly what a Marxian analysis, and lessons taken from the historical materialist perspective, might add.

TURNING DISABLEMENT INTO A WEAPON

What can we learn from the historical analysis provided here? How should we orient our organising and praxis? Let us first be clear about some key concepts and the ways they can be useful for either reproducing or challenging the dominant order. One initial insight that this historical analysis makes possible is that capital requires a certain ambiguity in beliefs about mental illness and disablement. On the one hand, it requires us to believe in mental illness and disablement just enough to justify the maintenance of a surplus class, and to be able to incarcerate divergent people who have not committed any recognised crime. This latter tendency is what the anti-psychiatrists saw and sought to challenge. But capital also requires us to be sceptical enough about the reality of mental illness and disablement so that it can get away with not providing health-care or support for the majority of those who need it. This is where many of the anti-psychiatrists got, and get, their analysis wrong. For in seeking to render recognition of mental illness or disability invalid as such, the Szaszian anti-psychiatrists produced a discourse that is enormously helpful for capital. For a mass cultural scepticism of the reality of mental illness nicely feeds into the need of state and capital to deny help where such help would fail to maximise profit.

It is also worth mentioning contemporary 'critical psychiatry'. This newer approach, which has become a small and relatively mainstream industry led by non-disabled clinical professionals, draws on the philosophical basis of anti-psychiatry but shifts from abolition to reformism. It mainly focuses on seeking to erase recognition of mental illness or disability, and instead frames diagnoses like ADHD or PTSD as mere 'distress', in a form of disability denial that is no less useful for capital than were its Szaszian predecessors. A good example of this approach is the work of James Davies. While he identifies some genuine harms of psychiatry, his own work goes back towards a moral model of disability, where distress is primarily understood as a potential for learning and growth. While suffering can of course sometimes allow growth, this orientation is a political dead end, and seems more likely to be used to justify the needs of the masses to suffer than to justify alleviating our suffering. Moreover, while Davies has correctly identified some of the harmful effects of neoliberal capitalism specifically, he still defends capitalism as such while very quickly dismissing attempts to develop communism.[4]

Given these practices and commitments, this clinician-led form of bourgeois reformism seems incompatible with a neurodivergent-led politics of emancipation.

With this in mind, it is worth considering that there are other traditions, not yet clarified here, which embraced politicised conceptions of mental illness rather than rejecting recognition of illness as such. Writing in the 1950s, for instance, Frantz Fanon saw mental illness as real illness, but also held it to be largely socially caused by inequality, colonialism, racism, and other social factors.[5] He sought to develop this into anti-racist praxis, which could be usefully synthesised with neurodiversity paradigm approaches. More recent efforts to decolonise mental health continue in Fanon's tradition. On the account of Mimi Khúc, for instance, this requires not just material decolonisation, but also a questioning and interrogation of manners in which 'larger forces and institutions have told us what counts as mental health and what counts as suffering'.[6] Decolonising efforts such as these tend to acknowledge that mental health is real but resist the imposition of hegemonic Western narratives and responses to such experiences.

Beyond decolonising efforts, the radical group the Socialist Patients Collective, active in West Germany in the 1970s, also saw mental illness as an undeniable fact. But for them it was primarily caused by societal factors, and they argued that illness was the only possible way of life under capitalism. They embraced the use of certain therapies and medications, but, as Adler-Bolton and Vierkant write, 'felt that, above all else, care should be self-directed and synergetic, a dual dialectic between doctor and patient working in collaboration and producing forms not just of care but also of solidarity'.[7] Alongside this, they sought to build a 'People's University' where treatments would be developed not for profit but on principles of collective self-determination. This challenge to the physician and researcher class, coupled with a commitment to ending capitalism, also provides a stark alternative to bourgeois and denialist mental health politics.

It is also worth emphasising the significance of the British Marxist Peter Sedgwick, whose critique of Szasz we have already mentioned.

In his 1982 book *PsychoPolitics*, Sedgwick critiqued what he rightly identified as the dualism of the anti-psychiatrists. Instead, he argued that recognising the reality of mental illness *as illness* was currently necessary for making demands from the state while also emphasising the need for alternative community organisation of mental health resources beyond the state apparatus. Given the failings of contemporary bourgeois critical psychiatry, there has been a resurgence of interest in Sedgwick in recent years, with two new editions of *PsychoPolitics* being published in the past decade. A Sedgwickian politics has recently been defended by scholar-activists such as Hel Spandler and Mark Cresswell.[8] This approach also has some overlap with contemporary radical survivor groups such as Recovery In the Bin, who call for 'a robust "Social Model of Madness, Distress & Confusion", placing mental health within the context of social justice and the wider class struggle.'[9] The radical mental health magazine *Asylum* has also resisted harmful binary thinking about mental health, taking a nuanced and pluralistic approach that holds space for recognition of illness and disability, consistent with the Sedgwickian tradition. Similarly, albeit more influenced by French post-structuralists, the social theorist Mark Fisher called for a politicisation of depression as a pathology definitive of the post-Fordist era.[10] This alternative British tradition ultimately affirms the need for and right to treatments while simultaneously aiming at breaking the centring of the needs of capital in treatment production. It promotes a form of abolitionism, but where the abolition is of social control rather than the recognition of unwellness or the right to treatment.

My understanding of Neurodivergent Marxism follows in these traditions, while departing on some specifics. Clearly, pathologisation can sometimes be wrongful and harmful, and in such cases should be resisted. But attempts to deny the reality of mental illness or disability *as such* are no less harmful. At best, they waste huge effort swapping terms (e.g. 'illness' for 'distress') without improving material conditions, while at worst they provide justification for a mass cultural denial of recognition of disablement, or state denial of the requirement to provide support. By contrast, the

Socialist Patients Collective's manifesto was titled *Turn Illness into a Weapon*, and they precisely called for the use of illness to demand resources and support while also calling for the 'sick proletariat' to fight against capitalist domination. In line with this example, Neurodivergent Marxism, as I understand it – at least at the current historical moment – seeks to turn both neurodivergent disablement and illness into sites of organisation and resistance to the system that necessitates both the production and harm of both neurodivergents and neurotypicals. In doing this, we should not seek to unwisely erase ancient concepts of mental illness, which as we have seen were recognised globally, as such. Rather, we must work towards breaking the associations between health, normality, and productivity. Challenging the biomedical and psychological understandings and their ideological functions, yet without denying the reality of mental illness or disablement, will be necessary for constructing new ways of recognising illness and disablement in such a manner that nonetheless resists eugenic ideology and pressure.

My understanding of Neurodivergent Marxism also sits in a realist and materialist tradition of disability studies, which sees disablement as always relationally produced between bodyminds and the world. This does not deny that there can be a pathological aspect to some forms of disability, which may require medical assistance. Indeed, it demands the right to access medical care as and where it is useful. But it resists the idea that disability is merely an individual problem, a mere mechanical breaking of the body or mind to always be mechanically fixed. As we have seen, our conceptions of ability, impairment, normality, and so forth change in different contexts. This is in part as more people actually become disabled or non-disabled, in relation to each other – compared to the norm – and to their environments. It is vital to remain realists about disability in this historical moment since just as with illness, there is a huge administrative and ideological pressure to obscure or erase recognition of disability. After all, recognising disability and how it is continually reproduced by the dominant mode of production implies recognition of the state's responsibility to provide support, for as long as the state persists.

On this view, neurodivergent disabilities such as autism or ADHD are not random clusters of traits, grouped together by psychiatric whim, as many liberal critical analyses of psychiatry suggest. Neither are they mere identities, as liberal neurodiversity proponents have suggested. Rather, they are what Sartre called 'serial collectives', that is, collectives of people that tend to share certain experiences and problems given objective relations with material conditions.[11] As we have seen in this book, our current disabilities emerged, certain clusters of traits became salient as disabilities, because of objective material relations emerging from the development of the Empire of Normality. This, however, does not mean that normality and divergence are not real: it only means that their reality is socially and materially constituted, and hence can be altered only through material change.

I do not mean to suggest that this is the final analysis of these issues. These are preliminary suggestions for the current historical moment. For now, my aim is not to work out exactly which classifications are valid or where the boundary between health and illness should lie. Such boundaries are not, and cannot be, fixed. They are relative to time and place and change as people and contexts change. Neither is my aim to suggest that such boundaries should never be challenged. To the contrary, I think they constantly require challenging, when it comes to both bodily and mental illness. For disablement and pathologisation occurs through colonial and capitalist logics, and often reproduces their valuations. Our analysis will thus assume that disability and illness are facts, even if they always arise in social and ideological contexts and even if the boundaries are necessarily shifting and obscure. It is only in accepting these as real that we can begin to effectively organise to change reality as it is currently constituted.

EXTRACTIVE ABANDONMENT

To recap, so far, we have explicitly used two aspects of a Marxian analysis. The first is the materialist approach to history, which views human consciousness and agency as significantly constituted yet also constrained by the broader economic, social, and material conditions and relations of the specific age. This has helped us see how modern conceptions of normality and productivity have arisen and changed how we think about health. We have also drawn on and developed Marx's conception of alienation, which shows how material conditions can be harmful to us and stratify us into hierarchies. This has helped us understand rising levels of mental illness or disablement in the modern world.

But a Marxian analysis offers more than just materialism. Marx also saw the potential for historical change arising dialectically, from contradictions in our material relations. In the period in which he was writing, recall, the key conflict he saw was between the capitalist class and the workers. As I have noted previously, for Marx, it was in the fact that value was developed collectively by the workers, but then accumulated by a tiny number of capitalists, that the possibility of a new synthesis lay. He saw that the capitalist drive for ever-increasing expansion constantly led to the need for new machinery and technology. In turn, he suggested, this would lead to increased worker deskilling and thus increased alienation. Highlighting this was important for Marx as he believed that this was unsustainable, and that once they became more aware of their situation, workers would be more likely to organise and resist. His theory thus both began in praxis and in turn sought to help to make future praxis more efficient.

We can see similar contradictions when it comes to disability. In this regard, newer materialist analyses have been most notably developed by activists and scholars such as Martha Russell, Jasbir Puar, Artie Vierkant, and Beatrice Adler-Bolton. These take us far beyond the oversimplifications sometimes associated with the traditional social model. On the one hand, as Martha Russell stresses, a Marxian analysis helps us see how capital and the state *need* a surplus population to act as a reserve army of workers. Notably, for Marx, since capitalists compete to produce, capitalism is inherently prone to crises of overproduction. This therefore often requires pushing some of the working class into the surplus population. Moreover, increased automation, driven by the most fundamental logics of capitalism, also continually pushes more of the population into the surplus. Yet, capitalism also often has periods of growth, which requires having a surplus to draw on. This reserve army must also be ready to be called upon in times of sickness, war, and so forth.

Thus, the existence of a surplus population is no less necessary for capitalism than is the existence of workers, since capitalism both creates an ever-expanding surplus population while also relying on them to act as a reserve army. Put another way, disabled people – who make up much of the surplus – need to exist for capitalism to exist, and are hence part of what is both produced by, and sustains, the system. So it is not just that the capitalist class also often finds ways to profit off the surplus class through a variety of industries built around the management and confinement of the surplus. It is also that the capitalist class both creates the surplus, and often needs them for the possibility of growth at all. For every time there is a possibility of growth, this suddenly requires more workers, and for them to be read a surplus population has to be maintained. On this view, then, it is not just the case that certain environments, especially when driven by capitalist logics, are disabling for people with impairments. It is also that capitalist logics both produce and require disablement, which is itself primarily determined in relation to the needs of capital at any given time.

The association between capitalism and health is complex, and has been further clarified by Adler-Bolton and Vierkant in their book *Health Communism: A Surplus Manifesto*. Here I have primarily focused on how capitalism led to a conflation of health with both normality and productivity. But there is more to say. Adler-Bolton and Vierkant emphasise how capitalism requires health, to some extent, for productivity. At the same time, it must pathologise surplus populations while mining them for productivity through industries of administration in order to extract profit from their ill health. And the central aim of this is not to improve the prospects of thriving for members of the surplus class, but rather for capitalists to profit from the ongoing maintenance of their unwellness alongside the exploitation of care workers.

The overall disposition of the capitalist political economy of health consists in what they call *extractive abandonment*. That is, capitalism both creates and extracts from the surplus class while simultaneously abandoning them. This allows Adler-Bolton and Vierkant to frame the surplus population as a class (rather than a subset of the working class). Importantly, this goes beyond a social model analysis, which frames disablement as oppression imposed by barriers. More than this, a political economy characterised by extractive abandonment of the surplus class must build industries to administer surplus populations in order to mine their oppressed status for profit while also extracting surplus value from workers at these institutions. We see this, for instance, in the multi-billion dollar Applied Behaviour Analysis industry, which does little to help most autistic individuals subjected to it, and harms many, but which continues to exist and grow because so much profit is made through it. Considering how the overall disposition of the political economy is one of extractive abandonment, this helps explain why this industry has been able to continue its expansion despite mass resistance from autistic activists.

TOWARDS NEURODIVERGENT POWER

With the analysis presented in this book, however, I argue that we see a more specific orientation of extractive abandonment when it comes to not just neurodivergence but also neurodiversity at the group level. Consider, on the one hand, how vital neurodiversity at the group level is for production. Part of what follows from adopting a neurodiversity paradigm lens is the recognition that mental functioning and thus production emerges from our neurological diversity at the group level. No human is capable of doing much alone, or is wholly independent, and everything we do relies to varying extents on people who think differently having produced at least some part of what each of us uses. Moreover, even those most valued in the neuronormative hierarchies of capitalism cannot produce except in tandem with those less valued. At the level of the team, the company, the corporation, whole industries, nations, or the economic system itself, neurodiversity – that is, diversity in cognitive and emotional functioning – is required for capitalism to continue at all.

This is not a mere theoretical claim. There are multiple historical and scientific studies that support this. For instance, one study found that including one person with ADHD in a group makes that group much better at creative problem-solving at the group level.[12] Other studies have found that increased cognitive diversity at the group level makes groups better at adapting to changing environments.[13] Marx himself noted that capitalism functioned in part by what he called 'the general intellect'[14] – the combined intellect of all humanity – and we can now add that the general intellect requires neurodiversity at the general level as well as in more local groups.

It is similarly notable that capitalism always requires surplus forms of neurodivergence ready for the cognitive requirements of tomorrow. As Marx noted, capitalism brings the constant revolution of the means of production – of technology, machinery, and so forth. But because of this, it constantly needs different kinds of minds to be ready for whatever comes next. Recall, as Harvey Blume wrote in his seminal neurodiversity article: 'Who can say what form of wiring will prove best at any given moment? Cybernetics and computer culture, for example, may favor a somewhat autistic cast of mind'.[15] While it has now become something of a stereotype to say autistic people are good with maths or computers, this is true in at least some cases. And where autistic people are not good with computers, many others provide important skills due to the various cognitive traits associated with the autistic population.

Yet despite capital both needing and constantly extracting from neurodivergent cognition, it simultaneously abandons neurodivergent people. This begins at birth, when neurodivergent infants are framed as tragedies, and continues in schools, which are still often based on eugenicist logics and forms of segregation. From there it continues in adulthood, whether in workplace discrimination or in the mass incarceration of neurodivergent people, in prisons and then nursing homes. This social subjugation is then reified through psychological and biomedical research, thus continually cementing the naturalisation of capitalist cognitive hierarchies.

These contradictions are important to bear in mind as they help us understand how capitalism requires neurodiversity, and neurodivergence, even while devaluing and seeking to control it. To be clear, I am not in any way suggesting that we should value neurodivergence because it contributes to collective functioning. Rather, my point is that recognising these factors is helpful for starting to apprehend how capitalism devalues neurodivergence even by its own logics. It is equally useful for recognising the power neurodivergent people have if we organise in great enough numbers to resist. While we are individually disabled, we have collective cognitive power – itself a product of our neurological diversity – that could be harnessed no less than the collective power of the working class to combat the dominant order.

It is worth considering how the proponent of a liberal neurodiversity approach might respond to what I have just suggested. The question they might raise here regards whether, if capital does *in fact* need both neurodivergence and collective neurodiversity, then there could be room for neurodivergent emancipation within a capitalist framework. That is, it could be argued that since capitalism and the state currently devalue neurodivergent people even from within the logics of capitalism, then the issue is more about misrecognition than political economy. In this argument, raising awareness that capital requires neurodivergence just as it requires neurotypicality could provide grounds for developing a revaluation and new recognition of neurodivergence within a capitalist system. If this were possible, it might seem like a good basis for cultivating neurodivergent liberation without changing the deeper structures of society.

Indeed, this seems to be precisely the implicit assumption guiding much equality, diversity, and inclusion work on neurodiversity, which focuses on recognising neurodivergent 'strengths' to help get more neurodivergent people into work. It is also worth noting that Singer's concept of an 'ecological society' that constructs niches is, while being opposed to the ideology of normality, still perfectly compatible with capitalist logics. After all, if capital and the state can construct niches to help neurodivergent people into work, they can then extract surplus value from neurodivergent labour. As and when this is economically viable there is room for expanding capitalist neuronormativity to incorporate some minds currently positioned as neurodivergent, to bring them out of the surplus through environmental construction that enables their functioning.

Yet I precisely do not think this will lead to liberation in any meaningful sense, at least not for any but the most privileged neurodivergent people. It is not just that this approach will inevitably exclude those with disabilities that require more immediate support, who will remain discriminated against in the surplus, segregated, and controlled. In this, it will only reform the pathology paradigm, making it marginally more inclusive, rather than overcome it. Neither is it only that capital would likely only use this to increase the administration and control of neurominorities, pushing them towards ever-more refined brain-type specific roles that would increase predetermined specialisation and thus limit freedom.

It is also that there is a further neuronormative contradiction in capitalism that, I think, shows this will not free even those of us who are granted niches to be able to enter the workforce. For based on the historical analysis provided in previous chapters, capitalism, especially once it reaches a period where labour requires high-level cognitive or emotional processing, is increasingly disposed towards making us *all*, at the very least, either mentally ill or disabled. This includes those positioned as temporarily neurotypical, who it harms even if not quite so directly as neurodivergents.

To understand this, consider how, as we have seen from my historical analysis, capitalism always has a neurological in-group and an out-group, the boundaries of which shift. This shifting is largely in relation to perceived productive potential, but also in relation to consumer potential and whether any given person is susceptible to adopting the desires required for the needs of capital. We have seen that this harms those in the out-group through positioning them as surplus, but it is also harmful to the in-group, as it positions them as workers to be exploited until they finally become neurodivergent through burnout, illness, or cognitive decline.

In this, as we see most clearly in post-Fordist economies, capitalism puts each of us between two harmful conditions. Either it 'values' us, in which case it makes us workers and mercilessly exploits us, making us ill through the alienation such exploitation brings. Or, it disvalues us, making us disabled and discriminating against us as part of the surplus population. This often pushes us into poverty and positions us to be treated as disposable. However each of our minds is constituted, we are caught between these two options, neither good for us, and both harmful in different ways.

Many of us sit somewhere between these two extremes, or fall from one into the other at different points in our lives. Some enabled people in the working class become disabled and end up discarded in the surplus class. For instance, a worker who catches COVID-19 and develops Long Covid, due to their working conditions (say, an unventilated office where large numbers of workers are crammed together), may suddenly find themselves neurodivergent and disabled to the point of being unable to work. Indeed, many people temporarily shift to the surplus class simply due to burnout from overwork and stress. Others begin in the surplus class, with neurodivergent disabilities, but then find a niche job where they can thrive for a time, until alienation makes them ill. Overall the situation is one where mental health is elusive for most of us, many of us are in precarious and part-time employment, and the lines between worker and surplus become blurred.

It is important to stress how this is interlocked with the oppression of manual workers as much as cognitive workers, and that the divide is often blurred and superficial. Most importantly, cognitive and emotional exploitation in post-Fordist economies require the production and harm of disabled people in the global south. As Jasbir Puar notes, the very same technologies used in post-Fordist economies

produce vastly debilitated populations across the globe, from Chinese labourers in Apple factories who commit suicide, to wheelchair technology that enhances mobility developed in Israel [...] on the backs of Palestinian oppression and immobility, to the mountains of e-waste hand-sanded by the working poor in India, to the neocolonial extraction of minerals and natural substances from resource-rich areas for the purpose of manufacturing hardware.[16]

In this, the same working of the same system harms both cognitive workers in the imperial core and manual workers in the peripheries, albeit in different ways. Across the globe, even while bringing rapid progress in mechanistic medicine, capitalism is making workers ill.

This contradiction – being caught between alienation and disablement – does not just help clarify how liberation is impossible under the capitalist mode of production. It also shows us how the interests of the working class and the interests of the surplus class are one. Rather than the surplus being a drain on workers, as the dominant ideology suggests, the two are intimately connected, with members of each routinely having some small part in, or crossing over to, the other. Both neurodivergence and neurotypicality are a matter of proximity to a norm that changes in line with both global and local changes in the means of production, as well as any given person's current level of ability or debility. Neurotypicality is not just a temporary phase for any individual, but a phase whose continuation becomes more unlikely with each passing year as capitalism intensifies.

11
After normality

Following the October Revolution in 1917, Vladimir Lenin and the Bolsheviks began attempting to shift from a capitalist to a communist economic system. This was no easy thing. Russia was poor, in great turmoil, and under threat of invasion from Germany and other nearby nations. Neither were the Bolsheviks experienced in ruling a country. After all, they were revolutionaries, not career politicians. Their attempts thus had mixed success.

Bolshevik rule improved day-to-day life for millions, bringing state healthcare and important reforms for disabled people. Yet despite their attempts to move beyond capitalism, the Bolshevik state never established communism. Rather, the Soviet Union took a form that some have called 'state capitalism'. Marx himself had seen communism as requiring the withering away of the state, and workers in control of their own workplaces. By contrast, the workspaces of the Soviet Union were state-controlled. Lenin himself had seen this as a brief transitional stage, preferable to market capitalism but still a form of capitalist domination. But when Joseph Stalin became state leader following Lenin's death in 1924, the new leader soon gave up on shifting beyond state capitalism. Instead, Stalin simply declared that communism had been achieved, despite this going against what Marx and Lenin had suggested.

In this context, the emphasis on production continued. And especially given the continuation of market capitalism over much of the world, there was still an emphasis on competition, albeit this time competition with the capitalists. At the same time, as the Lithuanian Marxist Raya Dunayevskaya argued as far back as 1941, alienation was maintained within these Soviet relations of production. In her own words, the 'determining factor in analysing the class nature of a society is not whether the means of production are the private property of the capitalist class or are state-owned' but 'whether they are monopolized and alienated from the direct producers'. With this in mind, she went on, in the Soviet Union 'there exists the real economic relation of state-capitalist-exploiter to the propertyless exploited'.[1]

As it shifted into an industrial state capitalist economy, biomedicine, psychiatry, and psychology in the Soviet Union remained within the pathology paradigm, and the broader Empire of Normality persisted. It was not just that the physician class refused to give up their power, or that these professions were used to pathologise political dissidents and for social control more generally, much as in the rest of the world. It was also that the idea of individual ability as compared to the norm, and the ideology of normality, still dominated. With very limited knowledge or analysis of neurodivergent oppression among the Bolsheviks, the Empire of Normality was not recognised as something that had to be destroyed in the course of the revolution.

Indeed, Pavlov himself, the father of behaviourism, was lauded by Lenin specifically for his contribution to normalisation. In 1921 Lenin declared the 'tremendous importance' of Pavlov's work to the 'working people of the world'[2] and provided funding for Pavlov's work in the hope of creating a new standardised Soviet man. In turn, Lenin embraced Taylor's scientific management of workers, which was adopted in Soviet Russia in the 1920s. The workers of the Soviet Union were, then, while spared from the harshest inequality of market capitalism, were not only lacking control of their workspaces. They were also being actively controlled to maximise production at all costs, which would have bought compulsory neuronormativity much as was found in the United States. This as much as anything else makes it clear that this attempt to move beyond capitalism never got past state capitalism, thus maintaining neuronormative domination despite radically decreasing economic inequality.

A particularly memorable example of pathology paradigm ideology concerns Lenin himself. After Lenin died in 1924, Stalin commissioned the creation of the Institute of the Brain. The aim of this institute was primarily to examine Lenin's brain with the hope of unlocking the secrets of his genius. As Victor Sebestyen details, Soviet scientists 'began the process of comparing Lenin's brain with those of "ordinary people"' as well as with 'the brains of other high achievers'.[3] This went on for a whole decade, at great expense, during which time Lenin's brain was preserved using formaldehyde and alcohol. It was chopped and sliced into parts which were then analysed in relation to the average over the following years. As it turned out, however, this project was the product of ideology, and a significant waste of resources. As the decade-long project came to an end it was reported, as Sebestyen summarises, the key finding was that 'Lenin's brain was fairly ordinary. An average male brain weighs between 1,300 and 1,400 grams; Lenin's was 1,340 grams'.

This is not to say that Bolshevik and Soviet approaches to normality were identical to those seen elsewhere. Initially, there had been less enthusiasm for eugenics in Russia than in Western European nations. As Nikolai Krementsov has detailed,[4] in the latter half of the nineteenth century, the Russian Empire largely lacked the socio-economic conditions, such as urbanisation, over-population, and an influential aristocracy, that had brought a growth of interest in eugenics elsewhere. In fact, eugenic research expanded in Russia only following the 1917 Revolution. Bolshevik scientists then came to distinguish between what they called 'bourgeois' eugenics and 'proletarian' eugenics. But these were relatively similar in practice, and this was in turn criticised by anti-eugenicist Marxists, who suggested the focus should be on healthcare and education rather than biological control. Overall, support for eugenics was no more or less widespread in the Soviet Union than it was elsewhere. And beyond the Soviet Union, as late as 1934 Leon Trotsky, who by then had become a fierce critic of Stalin, still stressed hope for the application of 'genuine scientific methods to the problem of eugenics' in the United States.[5] Ultimately, much as we have seen elsewhere, in Soviet Russia, and among Marxists more broadly, it was only following the Second World War that an open commitment to eugenics became widely seen as tainted by Fascism, and thus less acceptable. But even then, the ideology has continually re-emerged on the left as elsewhere on the political spectrum, with imagined utopian futures often being based on eugenicist logics that construct the ideal as a world that reinforces rather than challenges the equation between productivity and health.

It is not my aim to go into detail about the merits and limitations of Soviet policy or attempts to develop proletarian sciences. That attempt was highly complex and ambitious, and deserves much more careful attention than I can provide here. I only want to stress how just moving beyond currently dominant forms of capitalism, or just decreasing inequality, will not necessarily end the Empire of Normality. We must learn from the mistakes made by past attempts, and remember that since new economic systems grow out of the conditions imposed by older ones, it is likely that any attempt to develop towards post-capitalism will retain at least some elements of the apparatus I have called the Empire of Normality.

Indeed, many more recent speculations about the possibility of capitalism developing into a post-capitalist society – for instance through the use and democratisation of information technology – contain little or no consideration of neurodivergent oppression, or of how we might seek to minimise it in such new societal organisations. Without this, we have every reason to believe that these attempts too will retain elements of the apparatus that underpins and necessitates the production, scientific reification, and control of neurodivergence.

ESCAPING NORMALITY

The first thing we must do to combat the Empire of Normality is to further develop an analysis of its nature and workings, and to build a critique of these into our imagining of what a post-capitalist society might look like. Our future theory and praxis must work towards this end, if we do not want neuronormative domination to persist and even worsen. After all, especially given the re-emergence of fascist governments and oligarchies across the world in recent decades, there is every possibility that whatever comes after capitalism could be even worse.

As to the possibility of a form of communism, or post-capitalism, that goes beyond the Empire of Normality, it is not yet clear what this might look like. As I have already said, I have not sought here to propose a strategy or set of policies to alleviate the current situation. At the current historical moment, it seems to me, eugenic and capitalist ideologies are still so hegemonic, we are only just beginning to be able to glimpse signposts towards possible ways out. What this will turn out to look like will only be determined through mass consciousness-raising, critique, and collective imagining. This will be a mass theoretical, scientific, political, and revolutionary project of many years or decades.

But with what I have argued in mind, there are several things we can say, which hint at a variety of possibilities going forward. First, it is important that Marx's own writings reveal a commitment to an ideal that is directly opposed to neuronormative domination. While some readers have interpreted him as expressing a kind of essentialism about human nature and thriving, a closer reading reveals that his conception of human nature was much more flexible, and not fixed by any clear essence. As Paul Raekstad writes,

> Marx's conception of human development is inherently open-ended (because it's not evaluated in terms of any predetermined yardsticks), [and] pluralistic (because it acknowledges that there are many different valuable ways to develop, and no particular vision of full or perfect development is imposed upon anyone).[6]

It is notable that this is in line with the core insight from neurodiversity theory, which is that human neurological development is, at the species level, always diverse, unfinished, and open-ended. In line with this, Marx's vision of the highest stage of communism was one where it moves from each according to their abilities to, ultimately each according to their needs. That is, the end goal is one where people are provided for and valued regardless of their individual ability. In this, there is certainly more room – and we must work on this over the coming years – to further develop a theoretical

Marxism that has the insights and commitments of the neurodiversity movement built into its core.

Ultimately, we must be militant in our demand to shift towards ways of organising and living that do not value humans by individual productivity, and which do not see us as machines to be upgraded in line with the economic requirements of capital at any given time. While capitalism has brought great increases in medical understanding and technology, these have too often been used more to reify capitalist neuronormativity than to aid human flourishing in all its diversity. A neurodivergent communism would be one where we live and work together, in a shared ecology, without discriminating against individuals for being divergent or unproductive.

To begin working towards this we must work through the contradictions I have identified in capitalism, orienting our theory and praxis to the points where capital's power ends up undermining its own future prospects. Some of this will regard work. In practice, Neurodivergent Marxism requires moving away from diversity consultants teaching companies how to exploit more neurodivergent workers, and towards neurodivergent workers organising *as neurodivergents* to radically change the structures and expectations of the workplace. In fact, this has already been happening more in recent years, where, anecdotally, I have been told of many emerging neurodivergent-led groups forming to change their own workplaces. Neurodivergent trade unionists such as Janine Booth have begun working on how to make unions more neurodivergence-inclusive and more directed towards focusing on the needs of neurodivergent people.[7] More efforts to build neurodivergent-led cooperatives will also help build new ways and modes of working and relating, less tainted by the focus on profit over working conditions. A mass effort in this direction is important because it will not just increasingly change how work is organised and understood, but make it more open to many of those neurodivergents who are currently in the surplus, thus providing more organising power for more disabled people in the long run.

We can also already say that an integrated surplus class must organise *as surplus* alongside the workers of the world, and workers must orient their theory and praxis to include critique of eugenic ideology and the liberation of the surplus. It is not just that the combined forces of both will likely be necessary for realising the possibility of building a post-capitalist world. It will also be necessary for imagining one that does not just reproduce the Empire of Normality in a different way.

A transitional politics that centres the surplus and, crucially, finds ways to empower the surplus *as surplus*, will need to take different forms to traditional union organising, which is based on the threat of withholding regular waged labour. This could take various forms. It may be that unions can incorporate more mechanisms to support members of the surplus who are only sporadically employed to withhold labour, as historically, for instance, striking dockworkers in Britain, who were paid by the day, managed. Alternatively, it may be that demand for the implementation of a Universal Basic Income gives those members of surplus who have never worked more economic power – primarily the power to withhold as consumers but also to organise towards direct action – regardless of whether they can withhold labour.

Equally, it is worth noting Marxist-Leninist vanguardism, where a party led by workers seeks to raise revolutionary consciousness. An interesting recent event was the short-lived organisation Red Fightback, active in the United Kingdom between 2018 and 2023. While this organisation split due to problems with several members of the leadership, it also did important community work, and it is interesting to consider it as the first Marxist-Leninist political party to have an explicit commitment to ending neurodivergent oppression. Many members of the leadership were also openly neurodivergent and queer. In this, it has at least some overlap with the Black Panthers as it developed in the 1970s, as a Marxist-Leninist party that despite initial problems, later strove to become more intersectional in its efforts. It seems likely that we will see more neurodivergent Marxist-Leninist organisations in the coming years, especially as neuronormativty continues to become increasingly restrictive. This may be key in raising the consciousness of a broader neurodivergent movement that cuts across the working and surplus classes.

Neurodivergent Marxism also requires building on existing elements within mental health politics. When it comes to the various psych disciplines, we should not think that the abolition of coercion is impossible just because the abolitionist attempts from the 1960s and 1970s largely failed. They failed, as we saw, because there were not usually better alternatives, leading to many former asylum inmates ending up homeless or in prison. Moreover, Szaszianism was designed to work this way, and ultimately it was the broader shift to neoliberalism that allowed Szaszianism to become dominant as a purported counter-narrative to biomedical psychiatry. Yet this does not imply that other forms of abolitionism are not worth pursuing. These, to be successful, will likely need to be based more on the approach of the Basaglians, the Sedgwickians, and the Socialist Patient's Collective, all of which avoid the Szaszian and bourgeois critical psychiatry shift to disability denial and Hayekian moralism. We should aim to abolish coercion and harm, and the power of the physician class, while steadfastly protecting recognition of disability or illness alongside the need for housing, resources, support, and services. These services must be both radically changed and increased, in ways that centre the needs of those who need them, while mass community building must take place beyond the scope of state support.

At the level of scientific research, the continued construction of neurodiversity paradigm science requires new methods for measurement and analysis, the centring of neurodivergent perspectives, the use of social and ecological models of functioning, and a politicised understanding of neurodivergent disablement. This science will need to be led by and for neurodivergents, especially those who are multiply marginalised. This will be vital not just for breaking the grip of the pathology paradigm, but also for constructing new knowledges that will help guide us towards new forms of societal organisation and ways of living.

This also raises the importance of decolonising neurodiversity theory and research. While neurodiversity theory can certainly fit well with anti-racist politics, the perspectives that have been centred so far are of proponents (of a range of ethnicities) in the Global

North. It thus reflects the perspectives and concerns of those people. In the past few years, neurodiversity theory has increasingly been adopted and adapted across much of the majority world – from Chile to Kenya – and this seems like it will continue in the coming years, since global capitalism produces similar forms of debility, disability, and illness everywhere. This will change and challenge neurodiversity theory, allowing it to further develop in new directions that are led by and reflect the needs of different people in different local contexts. The attempt to build a neurodiversity paradigm by those of us in the Global North must therefore remain open and flexible enough to be adapted or superseded by those of us in the global south. Our neurodivergent praxis must also be internationalist in its orientation, aiming to destroy the eugenic borders that structure and limit movement globally.

A radical politics of neurodivergent conservation is also consistent with a radical politics of environmental conservation. After all, it has been the same logics, the same system, that has ravaged the biodiversity of the planet as has sought to eliminate the neurological diversity of humanity. And neurodivergent liberation is no less intertwined with the liberation of those of us who diverge from gendered and sexual norms, those oppressed by patriarchy, and those with bodily disabilities. For the ideals of normality and supernormality, as we have seen, grew together and are intimately intertwined with not just racial capitalism but also a range of interlocking systems of domination, out of which the Empire of Normality arose. Our Neurodivergent Marxism must work towards building an understanding of all of this, for there is no liberation without collective liberation.

It is vital to say here that some neurodivergent disablement and illness will always exist, and that imagined worlds where they do not exist at all are fascistic fantasies. But mass neurodivergent disablement and constant, widespread anxiety, panic, depression, and mental illness, combined with systemic discrimination of neurodivergent people, is a problem specific to the current historical era. Hegemonic neuronormative domination, in other words, is a key problem of our time. For the Empire of Normality, and in turn the pathology paradigm, emerged in the context of capitalist logics, but have now become pervasive and partially distinct systems of domination in their own rights.

I have tried to write a book that helps clarify some of the broader contexts that led to the problems so many of us continually experience. This helps us understand why the neurodiversity movement arose, and what neurodivergent liberation might require. In this, I hope to have contributed some small part to a collective project of consciousness-raising, in such a way that will help us orient our theory and praxis over the coming years. As I have acknowledged, this is of course incomplete, and is just one small step in a greater, collective march towards a new world. But what I hope to have shown, ultimately, is that at this historical moment, the collective building of a mass anti-capitalist politics of neurodiversity will be necessary for not just neurodivergent liberation but also for our broader efforts towards collective liberation.

Together, then, we must work towards a future world beyond the Empire of Normality. It is true that this is not a future that we can yet properly comprehend. For ideology still hangs everywhere around us, like an all-encompassing fog that impedes our ability to think and see. Yet as our collective consciousness grows, this fog will pass. Our strength too will grow as we organise as neurodivergent workers and members of the surplus class, across borders and sites of struggle globally. Our possibilities will expand as the old world falters and its structures crumble. We will then see a clear path with signposts towards a bright future. It is up to us to get there.

Notes

INTRODUCTION

1. Ginny Russell, Sal Stapley, Tamsin Newlove-Delgado, Andrew Salmon, Rhianna White, Fiona Warren, Anita Pearson, and Tamsin Ford. 'Time Trends in Autism Diagnosis over 20 Years: A UK Population-Based Cohort Study'. *Journal of Child Psychology and Psychiatry* 63, no. 6 (2021): 674–682. https://doi.org/10.1111/jcpp.13505

2. Dennis Campbell. 'UK Has Experienced "Explosion" in Anxiety Since 2008, Study Finds'. *The Guardian*, 14 September 2020, www.theguardian.com/society/2020/sep/14/uk-has-experienced-explosion-in-anxiety-since-2008-study-finds

3. Qingqing Liu, Hairong He, Jin Yang, Xiaojie Feng, Fanfan Zhao, and Jun Lyu. 'Changes in the Global Burden of Depression from 1990 to 2017: Findings from the Global Burden of Disease Study'. *Journal of Psychiatric Research* 126 (2020): 134–140. https://doi.org/10.1016/j.jpsychires.2019.08.002

4. Lee Knifton, and Greig Inglis. 'Poverty and Mental Health: Policy, Practice and Research Implications'. *BJPsych Bulletin* 44, no. 5 (2020): 193–196. http://doi.org/10.1192/bjb.2020.78

5. Kassiane Asasumasu. 2018. 'PSA from the Actual Coiner of "Neurodivergent"'. https://sherlocksflataffect.tumblr.com/post/121295972384/psa-from-the-actual-coiner-of-neurodivergent

6. Steve Graby. 'Neurodiversity: Bridging the Gap Between the Disabled People's Movement and the Mental Health System Survivors' Movement?' In *Madness, Distress and the Politics of Disablement*. Bristol, UK: Policy Press, 2015. https://doi.org/10.51952/9781447314592. ch016

7. Dennis Campbell. 'One in Four UK Prisoners has Attention Deficit Hyperactivity Disorder, Says Report'. *The Guardian*, 18 June 2022. www.theguardian.com/society/2022/jun/18/uk-prisoners-attention-deficit-disorder-adhd-prison

8. Kairi Kõlves, Cecilie Fitzgerald, Merete Nordentoft, Stephen James Wood, and Annette Erlangsen. 'Assessment of Suicidal Behaviors Among Individuals with Autism Spectrum Disorder in Denmark'.

JAMA Network Open 4, no. 1 (2021): 1–17. http://doi.org/10.1001/jamanetworkopen.2020.33565

9. 'Dialectical materialism' is the term that was preferred by Marxist-Leninists in the Soviet Union, while Western Marxists preferred to say 'historical materialism'. I will use these terms interchangeably here, and do not mean to signal adherence to either group.

10. Karl Marx. *The Karl Marx Library, Volume I.* Edited by Saul K. Padover. New York: McGraw Hill, 1972, 46.

11. Karl Marx. 'Estranged Labour'. *Economic and Philosophical Manuscripts of 1844. Marxists Internet Archive,* 1844. www.marxists.org/archive/marx/works/1844/manuscripts/labour.htm

12. Nabil Ahmed, Anna Marriott, Nafkote Dabi, Megan Lowthers, Max Lawson, and Leah Mugehera. *Inequality Kills: The Unparalleled Action Needed to Combat Unprecedented Inequality in the Wake of COVID-19.* Oxford: Oxfam, 2022. https://policy-practice.oxfam.org/resources/inequality-kills-the-unparalleled-action-needed-to-combat-unprecedented-inequal-621341/

13. Raya Dunayevskaya. 'The Union of Soviet Socialist Republics is a Capitalist Society'. *The Marxist-Humanist Theory of State Capitalism: Selected Writings.* Chicago: News and Letters, 1992. www.marxists.org/archive/dunayevskaya/works/1941/ussr-capitalist.htm

14. Herbert Marcuse. *Soviet Marxism: A Critical Analysis.* London and Aylesbury: Routledge & Kegan Paul, 1969.

15. Cedric J. Robinson. *Black Marxism: The Making of the Black Radical Tradition.* London: Penguin Modern Classics, 2021.

16. Arlie Russell Hochschild. *The Managed Heart: Commercialization of Human Feeling.* Berkeley: University of California Press, 2012.

17. Michael Oliver. *The Politics of Disablement.* London: Macmillan Education, 1990.

18. Joel Kovel. *The Enemy of Nature: The End of Capitalism or the End of the World?* New York: Zed Books, 2002.

CHAPTER 1

1. Debby Sneed. 'The Architecture of Access: Ramps at Ancient Greek Healing Sanctuaries'. *Antiquity* 94, no. 376 (August 2020): 1015–1029. https://doi.org/10.15184/aqy.2020.123

2. Plato. *Phaedrus.* Translated by Alexander Nehamas and Paul Woodruff. Indianapolis: Hackett, 1995.

3. Hippocrates. *Hippocratic Writings.* Translated by G. E. R. Lloyd, John Chadwick, and W. N. Mann. Harmondsworth: Penguin, 1984, 339.

4. They also recognised hysteria, although following earlier beliefs, this was seen as stemming not from neurological pathology, but rather from the womb 'wandering' around the body and upsetting its general balance. While there was no systemic oppression of disabled people as a whole, here we see an early example of patriarchal oppression through diagnosis, whereby women were prescribed marriage and regular sex as treatment for a wandering womb.

5. Simon Raper. 'The Shock of the Mean'. *Significance* 14, no. 6 (2017): 12. https://doi.org/10.1111/j.1740-9713.2017.01087.x

6. Andrew Scull. *Madness in Civilization: A Cultural History of Insanity, from the Bible to Freud, from the Madhouse to Modern Medicine.* Princeton: Princeton University Press, 2016, 28.

7. Scull, *Madness in Civilization*, 28.

8. Sheldon Watts. *Disease and Medicine in World History*. London: Routledge, 2003.

9. Alexus McLeod. 'Chinese Philosophy has Long Known that Mental Health is Communal'. *Psyche*, 1 June 2020. https://psyche.co/ideas/chinese-philosophy-has-long-known-that-mental-health-is-communal

10. René Descartes. *Meditations on First Philosophy with Selections from the Objections and Replies.* Translated by Michael Moriarty. Oxford: Oxford University Press, 2008, 60.

11. Theodor Ebert. 'Did Descartes Die of Poisoning?' *Early Science and Medicine* 24, 2 (2019): 142–185, https://doi.org/10.1163/15733823-00242P02

12. William Brockbank. *Portrait of a Hospital, 1752–1948 to Commemorate the Bi-Centenary of the Royal Infirmary, Manchester.* London: William Heinemann, 1952, 73.

13. Elizabeth I. 'An Act for the Relief of the Poor'. 1601. www.workhouses.org.uk/poorlaws/1601act.shtml

14. Buluda Itandala. 'Feudalism in East Africa'. *Utafiti: Journal of the Faculty of Arts and Social Sciences* 8, no. 2 (1986): 29–42.

15. Stephen Cave, and Kanta Dihal. 'Ancient Dreams of Intelligent Machines: 3,000 Years of Robots'. *Nature: Books and Arts*, 25 July 2018. www.nature.com/articles/d41586-018-05773-y#:~:text=The%20French%20philosopher%20Ren%C3%A9%20Descartes,the%20philosopher's%20death%20in%201650

16. Silvia Federici. *Caliban and the Witch: Women, the Body and Primitive Accumulation.* New York: Autonomedia, 2004.

17. Karl Marx. *Capital: A Critique of Political Economy, Volume III.* Translated by Ben Fowkes and David Fernbach. London: Penguin, 1990, 182.

18. Vic Finkelstein. 'Disability and the Helper/Helped Relationship'. In *Handicap in a Social World*, edited by Ann Brechin, Penny Liddiard, and John Swain. Sevenoaks: Hodder & Stoughton, 1981, 3. Reprinted at https://disability-studies.leeds.ac.uk/wp-content/uploads/sites/40/library/finkelstein-Helper-Helped-Relationship.pdf
19. David M. Turner, and Daniel Blackie. *Disability in the Industrial Revolution: Physical Impairment in British Coalmining, 1780–1880*. Manchester: Manchester University Press, 2018, 7.
20. Stefanie Hunt-Kennedy. 'Unfree Labor and Industrial Capital: Fitness, Disability, and Worth'. In *Between Fitness and Death*, 80–85. Champaign: University of Illinois Press, 2020. https://doi.org/10.5622/illinois/9780252043192.003.0004
21. Caitlin Rosenthal. 'Slavery's Scientific Management'. In *Slavery's Capitalism*, edited by Seth Rockman and Sven Beckert, 62–86. Philadelphia: University of Pennsylvania Press, 2016, 62.
22. Karl Marx. *Capital: A Critique of Political Economy, Volume I*. Translated by Ben Fowkes. London: Penguin Books, 1990, 523.

CHAPTER 2

1. Peter M. Cryle, and Elizabeth Stephens. *Normality: A Critical Genealogy*. Chicago: University of Chicago Press, 2018, 31–41.
2. Adolphe Quetelet. *A Treatise on Man and the Development of His Faculties*. Translated by R. Knox. Edited by T. Smibert. Cambridge: Cambridge University Press, 2014, 9–10. https://doi.org/10.1017/CBO9781139864909
3. Coreen McGuire. *Measuring Difference, Numbering Normal: Setting the Standards for Disability in the Interwar Period*. Manchester: Manchester University Press, 2020.
4. Quetelet, *Treatise on Man*, 99.
5. Allan V. Horwitz. *What's Normal? Reconciling Biology and Culture*. New York: Oxford University Press, 2016, 6.
6. Lennard J. Davis. *Enforcing Normalcy: Disability, Deafness, and the Body*. London: Verso, 1995, 26–27.
7. Amber Haque. 'Psychology from Islamic Perspective: Contributions of Early Muslim Scholars and Challenges to Contemporary Muslim Psychologists'. *Journal of Religion and Health* 43, no. 4 (2004): 357–377.
8. C. F. Goodey. *A History of Intelligence and 'Intellectual Disability': The Shaping of Psychology in Early Modern Europe*. Farnham: Ashgate, 2011, 221.
9. Roddy Sloarch. *A Very Capitalist Condition: A History and Politics of Disability*. London: Bookmarks, 2016, 57.

10. John Brydall. *Non Compos Mentis: Or, The Law Relating to Natural Fools*. London: Atkins, 1700, 9.
11. Simon Jarrett. *Those They Called Idiots: The Idea of the Disabled Mind from 1700 to the Present Day*. London: Reaktion Books, 2020, 24–71.
12. Quetelet himself contributed to this shift in his writings on what he called 'the statistics of the deranged', and 'diseases of the mind'. Nonetheless, while he described people with such disabilities as being 'in a direct ratio with civilisation', his research only included statistics about these people rather than about the nature *of* the normal mind as such. He charted, for instance, how many idiots made up the population of a country, the month in which they were most often born, the age of onset of insanity, and so forth. In my view, he did not, therefore, develop the concept of the normal mind, although he certainly paved the way for it.
13. James Straton. *Contribution to the Mathematic of Phrenology: Chiefly Intended for Students*. Aberdeen: William Russell, 1845, 4.
14. Straton, *Mathematic of Phrenology*, 19.
15. Stefanie Hunt-Kennedy. 'Imagining Africa, Inheriting Monstrosity: Gender, Blackness, and Capitalism in the Early Atlantic World'. In *Between Fitness and Death*, 13–38. Champaign: University of Illinois Press, 2020. https://doi.org/10.5622/illinois/9780252043192.003.0002
16. Fenneke Sysling. 'Phrenology and the Average Person, 1840–1940'. *History of the Human Sciences* 34, no. 2 (2021): 40. https://doi.org/10.1177/0952695120984070
17. Michel Foucault. *Madness and Civilization: A History of Insanity in the Age of Reason*. New York: Vintage Books, 2006.
18. Roy Porter. 'Foucault's Great Confinement'. *History of the Human Sciences* 3, no. 1 (1990): 47–54. https://doi.org/10.1177/095269519000300107
19. Henry Maudsley. *The Physiology and Pathology of the Mind*. New York: Appleton, 1867, 50.
20. Richard Keller. 'Madness and Colonization: Psychiatry in the British and French Empires, 1800–1962'. *Journal of Social History* 35, no. 2 (2001): 307.
21. Andrew Scull. 'Madness and Segregative Control: The Rise of the Insane Asylum'. *Social Problems* 24, no. 3 (1977): 344–345. https://doi.org/10.2307/800085
22. Scull, 'Madness and Segregative Control', 342.

CHAPTER 3

1. Charles Darwin. *On the Origin of Species by Means of Natural Selection, Or, The Preservation of Favoured Races in the Struggle for Life*. London: John Murray, 1859.

2. Francis Galton. *Hereditary Genius: An Inquiry into its Laws and Consequences.* London: Macmillan, 1869, 29.

3. Galton, *Hereditary Genius*, 66.

4. Francis Galton. *Memories of My Life.* London: Methuen, 1908, 290.

5. Alfred R. Wallace. Review of *Hereditary Genius, an Inquiry into its Laws and Consequences* by Francis Galton. *Nature* 1 (1870): 501–503. https://doi.org/10.1038/001501a0

6. Frederic William Farrar. 'Review of *Hereditary Genius* by Francis Galton'. *Fraser's Magazine* 2 (1870): 260.

7. Kurt Danziger. *Constructing the Subject: Historical Origins of Psychological Research.* Cambridge: Cambridge University Press, 1990, 56.

8. Francis Galton. 'The History of Twins, as a Criterion of the Relative Powers of Nature and Nurture'. *Fraser's Magazine* 12 (1875): 566.

9. Francis Galton. *Natural Inheritance.* 5th ed. New York: Macmillan, 1894.

10. Ian Hacking. *The Taming of Chance.* Cambridge: Cambridge University Press, 1990, 180.

11. Francis Galton. *Inquiries into Human Faculty and Its Development.* London: Everyman, 1907, 17–18. https://galton.org/books/human-faculty/SecondEdition/text/web/human-faculty4.htm#_Toc503102656

12. Donald Mackenzie. *Statistics in Britain 1865-1930 The Social Construction of Scientific Knowledge.* Edinburgh, Edinburgh University Press, 1981, 33.

13. Mackenzie, *Statistics in Britain*, 29.

14. Galton, *Inquiries into Human Faculty*, 36.

15. Lennard J. Davis. *Enforcing Normalcy: Disability, Deafness, and the Body.* London: Verso, 1995, 33.

16. Galton, *Inquiries into Human Faculty*, 35.

17. Galton, *Inquiries into Human Faculty*, 17.

18. Peter M. Cryle, and Elizabeth Stephens. *Normality: A Critical Genealogy.* Chicago: University of Chicago Press, 2018, 232.

19. Emil Kraepelin. *Memoirs.* Edited by Hanns Hippius, G. Peters, and Detlev Ploog. Berlin: Springer-Verlag, 1987, 55. https://doi.org/10.1007/978-3-642-71924-0

20. Danziger, *Constructing the Subject*, 118.

21. Emil Kraepelin. 'Ends and Means of Psychiatric Research'. *Journal of Mental Science* 68, no. 281 (1922): 134. https://doi.org/10.1192/bjp.68.281.115

22. Kraepelin, 'Ends and Means', 136.

23. Kraepelin, 'Ends and Means', 137.

24. Eugen Bleuler. *Textbook of Psychiatry*. Translated by A. A. Brill. New York: Macmillan, 1924, 214.

CHAPTER 4

1. Pauline M. H. Mazumdar. *Eugenics, Human Genetics and Human Failings: The Eugenics Society, Its Sources and its Critics in Britain*. London and New York: Routledge, 1992, x, 373.
2. Quoted in Roddy Sloarch. *A Very Capitalist Condition: A History and Politics of Disability*. London: Bookmarks, 2016, 97.
3. Stern, Alexandra Minna. 'Making Better Babies: Public Health and Race Betterment in Indiana, 1920–1935'. *American Journal of Public Health* 92, no. 5 (2002): 748. https://doi.org/10.2105%2Fajph.92.5.742
4. Sloarch, *Very Capitalist Condition*, 100.
5. Lennard J. Davis. *Enforcing Normalcy: Disability, Deafness, and the Body*. London: Verso, 1995, 27.
6. Sidney Webb. *The Difficulties of Individualism*. London: The Fabian Society, 1896, 6.
7. Stephen Heathorn. 'Explaining Russell's Eugenic Discourse in the 1920s'. *Russell: The Journal of Bertrand Russell Studies* 25, no. 2 (2005): 135. https://doi.org/10.15173/russell.v25i2.2083
8. Marie Carmichael Stopes. *Radiant Motherhood: A Book for Those Who Are Creating the Future*. London: G. P. Putnam's Sons, 1921.
9. Mark B. Adams. 'The Politics of Human Heredity in the USSR, 1920–1940'. *Genome* 31, no. 2 (1989): 879–884. https://doi.org/10.1139/g89-155
10. Chloe Campbell. *Race and Empire: Eugenics in Colonial Kenya*. Manchester: Manchester University Press, 2011, 11.
11. Robert Proctor. *Racial Hygiene: Medicine under the Nazis*. Cambridge, MA and London: Harvard University Press, 1988, 42.
12. E. Fuller Torrey, and Robert H. Yolken. 'Psychiatric Genocide: Nazi Attempts to Eradicate Schizophrenia'. *Schizophrenia Bulletin* 36, no. 1 (2010): 26–32. https://doi.org/10.1093/schbul/sbp097
13. John Elder Robison. 'Kanner, Asperger, and Frankl: A Third Man at the Genesis of the Autism Diagnosis'. *Autism* 21, no. 7 (2017): 5.
14. Robert Chapman. 'Did Gender Norms Cause the Autism Epidemic?' *Critical Neurodiversity*, 29 November 2016. https://criticalneurodiversity.com/2016/11/29/did-gender-norms-cause-the-autism-epidemic/
15. Henry Friedlander. *The Origins of Nazi Genocide: From Euthanasia to the Final Solution*. Chapel Hill and London: University of North Carolina Press, 1995, xii.

16. Nick Walker. 'Throw Away the Master's Tools: Liberating Ourselves from the Pathology Paradigm'. In *Loud Hands: Autistic People, Speaking.* Edited by J. Bascom, 225–237. Washington: Autistic Self Advocacy Network, 2012.

CHAPTER 5

1. Wilhelm Reich. *The Mass Psychology of Fascism.* New York: Orgone Institute Press, 1946.
2. Sigmund Freud. *The Psychopathology of Everyday Life.* Translated by James Strachey. Harmondsworth: Penguin Books, 1975.
3. Thomas Szasz. 'An Autobiographical Sketch'. In *Szasz Under Fire: The Psychiatric Abolitionist Faces His Critics.* Edited by Jeffrey A. Schaler, 1–28. Chicago: Open Court, 2004, 22–23.
4. Szasz, 'Autobiographical Sketch', 24.
5. Thomas Szasz. 'The Myth of Mental Illness'. *American Psychologist* 15, no. 2 (1960): 113–118. https://doi.org/10.1037/h0046535
6. Szasz, 'Myth of Mental Illness', 114.
7. Szasz, 'Myth of Mental Illness', 114.
8. Szasz, 'Myth of Mental Illness', 114.
9. To be sure, if underlying biological abnormality is found, Szasz was happy to say that the illness was genuine, and the pathology objective. In these cases, though, he thought that pathologisation was a purely scientific matter and that care of the now verified condition should be passed from psychiatry to neurology. Indeed, he noted, this is exactly what had tended to happen historically, such as when what had previously been known as general paralysis or paresis of the insane was found to be caused by syphilis in the 1890s. Without this, there was no justification for calling something an illness, thus placing those suffering under the power of doctors. At the time he was writing, there was also no known biological basis for any mental disorder – meaning that his argument posed a powerful challenge to the very core of psychiatry.
10. David G. Cooper. *Psychiatry and Anti-Psychiatry.* Abingdon: Routledge, 2001.
11. David G. Cooper ed. *The Dialectics of Liberation.* Harmondsworth: Penguin, 1968.
12. Michael E. Staub. *Madness is Civilisation: When the Diagnosis Was Social, 1948–1980.* Chicago and London: University of Chicago Press, 2011.
13. Staub, *Madness is Civilisation*, 110.

14. Judi Chamberlin. *On Our Own: Patient-Controlled Alternatives to the Mental Health System.* New York: Hawthorn Books, 1978.
15. Andrew Scull. *Desperate Remedies: Psychiatry's Turbulent Quest to Cure Mental Illness.* Cambridge, MA: Harvard University Press, 2022, 294.
16. John Foot. *The Man Who Closed the Asylums: Franco Basaglia and the Revolution in Mental Health Care.* London: Verso Books, 2015.
17. Peter Sedgwick. *Psychopolitics: Laing, Foucault, Goffman, Szasz, and the Future of Mass Psychiatry.* London: Unkant, 2015, 216.
18. Anne Parsons. *From Asylum to Prison: Deinstitutionalisation and the Rise of Mass Incarceration after 1945.* Chapel Hill: The University of North Carolina Press, 2018, 5.
19. Scull, *Desperate Remedies*, 291.
20. David C. Grabowski, Kelly A. Aschbrenner, Zhanlian Feng, and Vincent Mor. 'Mental Illness in Nursing Homes: Variations Across States'. *Health Affairs* 28, no. 3 (2009): 689–700. https://doi.org/10.1377/hlthaff.28.3.689
21. Andrew Scull. *Decarceration: Community Treatment and the Deviant – A Radical View.* Hoboken: Prentice-Hall, 1977.
22. Scull, *Desperate Remedies*, 290.
23. Liat Ben-Moshe. *Decarcerating Disability: Deinstitutionalization and Prison Abolition.* Minneapolis, Minnesota University Press, 2020.
24. Thomas Szasz. Letters to Friedrich August von Hayek, 1964–1983. *The Thomas S. Szasz, M.D. Cybercenter for Liberty and Responsibility.* www.szasz.com/hayek.html
25. Thomas Szasz. *Psychiatry: The Science of Lies.* New York: Syracuse University Press, 2008, 110.
26. Friedrich A. Hayek. *The Road to Serfdom: Text and Documents.* Definitive ed. Edited by Bruce Caldwell. Chicago: University of Chicago Press, 2007, 217.

CHAPTER 6

1. Karl Marx. *Grundrisse: Foundations of the Critique of Political Economy.* Translated by [Martin Nicolous]. Ayelsbury: Penguin Books, 1993, 287.
2. Edward Bernays. 'The Engineering of Consent'. *Annals of the American Academy of Political and Social Science* 250, no. 1 (1947): 119. https://doi.org/10.1177/000271624725000116
3. Max Horkheimer, and Theodor Adorno. *Dialectic of Enlightenment: Philosophical Fragments.* Edited by Gunzelin Schmid Noerr. Translated

by Edmund Jephcott. Stanford: Stanford University Press, 2002, 94–97.

4. Herbert Marcuse. *One-Dimensional Man: Studies in the Ideology of Advanced Industrial Society*. Boston: Beacon Press, 1964, 7.

5. Majia Holmer Nadesan. *Constructing Autism: Unravelling the 'Truth' and Understanding the Social*. London: Routledge, 2005, 58.

6. Ivan Pavlov. *The Work of the Digestive Glands*. London: Griffin, 1902.

7. John Watson. *Behaviorism*. New York: People's Institute, 1924, 104.

8. Burrhus Frederic Skinner. *The Behavior of Organisms*. New York: Appleton-Century-Crofts, 1938.

9. Burrhus Frederic Skinner. *Beyond Freedom and Dignity*. Bungay: Pelican, 1976.

10. Rebecca Lemov. *World as Laboratory: Experiments with Mice, Mazes, and Men*. New York: Hill and Wang, 2005.

11. Lemov, *World as Laboratory*, 54.

12. Lemov, *World as Laboratory*, 53.

13. Edward Hunter. 'Brain-Washing Tactics Force Chinese into Ranks of the Communist Party'. *Miami News*, 24 September 1950.

14. Lemov, *World as Laboratory*, 3.

15. Daniel Bell. 'The Study of Man: Adjusting Men to Machines'. *Commentary*, January 1947. www.commentary.org/articles/daniel-bell-2/the-study-of-man-adjusting-men-to-machines/

16. See, e.g. Burrhus Frederic Skinner. *Beyond Freedom and Dignity*. Bungay: Pelican, 1976, 154.

17. John Stewart. '"The Dangerous Age of Childhood": Child Guidance in Britain c.1918–1955'. *History & Policy*, 1 October 2012. www.historyandpolicy.org/policy-papers/papers/the-dangerous-age-of-childhood-child-guidance-in-britain-c.1918-1955

18. Dan Moser, and Allan Grant. 'Screams, Slaps and Love: A Surprising, Shocking Treatment Helps Fargone Mental Cripples'. *Life*, 7 May 1965, 90.

19. George Rekers, and Ivar Lovaas. 'Behavioral Treatment of Deviant Sex-Role Behaviors in a Male Child'. *Journal of Applied Behavior Analysis* 7, no. 2 (1974): 173–190. https://doi.org/10.1901/jaba.1974.7-173

20. Robert Whitaker. *Anatomy of an Epidemic: Magic Bullets, Psychiatric Drugs, and the Astonishing Rise of Mental Illness in America*. New York: Crown, 2010, 84.

21. Andrew Scull. *Madness in Civilization: A Cultural History of Insanity, from the Bible to Freud, from the Madhouse to Modern Medicine*. Princeton: Princeton University Press, 2016, 367.

CHAPTER 7

1. George H. W. Bush. 'Presidential Proclamation 6158'. *Library of Congress*, 17 July 1990. www.loc.gov/loc/brain/proclaim.html
2. American Psychiatric Association. *Diagnostic and Statistical Manual of Mental Disorders*. Washington DC: APA Press, 1952, 138–139.
3. American Psychiatric Association. *DSM-II: Diagnostic and Statistical Manual of Mental Disorders*. Washington DC: APA Press, 1968, 44.
4. Richard McNally. *What is Mental Illness?* Cambridge: Belknap Press, 2011, 24.
5. American Psychiatric Association. *DSM-III: Diagnostic and Statistical Manual*. Washington DC: APA Press, 1980, 6.
6. Robert L. Spitzer 'The Diagnostic Status of Homosexuality in DSM-III: A Reformulation of the Issues'. *American Journal of Psychiatry* 212, no. 2 (1981): 210–215. https://doi.org/10.1176/ajp.138.2.21, emphasis in original.
7. Christopher Boorse. 'On the Distinction Between Disease and Illness'. *Philosophy and Public Affairs* 5, no. 1 (1975): 49–68.
8. Nancy Andreasen. *The Broken Brain: The Biological Revolution in Psychiatry*. New York and London: Harper & Row, 1984, 8.
9. Ethan Watters. *Crazy Like Us: The Globalization of the Western Mind*. St Ives: Robison, 2011.
10. Robert Whitaker. *Anatomy of an Epidemic: Magic Bullets, Psychiatric Drugs, and the Astonishing Rise of Mental Illness in America*. New York: Crown, 2010, 8.
11. Stephen Taylor, Fizz Annand, Peter Burkinshaw, Felix Greaves, Michael Kelleher, Jonathan Knight, Clare Perkins, Anh Tran, Martin White, John Marsden. Dependence and Withdrawal Associated with Some Prescribed Medicines: An Evidence Review'. *Public Health England*, London. 2019. https://assets.publishing.service.gov.uk/government/uploads/system/uploads/attachment_data/file/940255/PHE_PMR_report_Dec2020.pdf
12. Emily Terlizzi, and Tina Norris. 'Mental Health Treatment Among Adults: United States, 2020'. *NCHS Data Brief* 419 (2021). https://dx.doi.org/10.15620/cdc:110593external icon
13. Adam Rogers. 'Star Neuroscientist Tom Insel Leaves the Google-Spawned Verily for [...] a Startup?' *Wired*, 11 May 2017. www.wired.com/2017/05/star-neuroscientist-tom-insel-leaves-google-spawned-verily-startup/?mbid=social_twitter_onsiteshare
14. Andrea Cipriani, Furukawa Toshi, Georgia Salanti, Anna Chaimani, Lauren Z. Atkinson, Yusuke Ogawa, Stefan Leucht, Henricus G. Ruhe, Erick H. Turner, Julian P. Higgins, Matthias Egger, Nozomi Takeshima,

Yu Hayasaka, Hissei Imai, Shinohara Kiyomi, Aran Tajika, John P. A. Ioannidis, and John R. Geddes 'Comparative Efficacy and Acceptability of 21 Antidepressant Drugs for the Acute Treatment of Adults with Major Depressive Disorder: A Systematic Review and Network Meta-Analysis'. *The Lancet* 391, no. 10128 (2018): 1357–1366. https://doi.org/10.1016/S0140-6736(17)32802-7

CHAPTER 8

1. David Harvey. *A Brief History of Neoliberalism*. Oxford: Oxford University Press, 2005, 2.
2. Harvey, *Brief History of Neoliberalism*, 3.
3. Margaret Thatcher. 'Interview for *Catholic Herald*, 5 December 1978'. *Margaret Thatcher Foundation*. www.margaretthatcher.org/document/103793
4. Margaret Thatcher. 'Nicholas Ridley Memorial Lecture'. Central London, 22 November 1996. *Margaret Thatcher Foundation*. www.margaretthatcher.org/document/108368
5. Iain Ferguson. *Politics of the Mind: Marxism and Mental Distress*. London: Bookmarks, 2017, 15–17.
6. Ferguson, *Politics of the Mind*, 16.
7. Karl Marx. 'Estranged Labour'. *Economic and Philosophical Manuscripts of 1844*. Marxists Internet Archive, 1844. www.marxists.org/archive/marx/works/1844/manuscripts/labour.htm
8. Charles Wright Mills. *White Collar: The American Middle Classes*. 50th anniversary ed. New York: Oxford University Press, 2002, 182–188.
9. Arlie Russell Hochschild. *The Managed Heart: Commercialization of Human Feeling*. Berkeley: University of California Press, 2012, 8.
10. Hochschild, *Managed Heart*, 7.
11. Hochschild, *Managed Heart*, 131.
12. Hochschild, *Managed Heart*, 54.
13. Yann Moulier Boutang. *Cognitive Capitalism*. Translated by Ed Emery. Cambridge: Polity Press, 2012, 50–57.
14. Franco Berardi. *The Soul at Work: From Alienation to Autonomy*. Los Angeles: Semiotext(e), 2009, 24.
15. Berardi, *Soul at Work*, 109.
16. Sami Timimi, Brian McCabe, and Neil Gardner. *The Myth of Autism: Medicalising Mens' and Boys' Social and Emotional Competence*. Basingstoke: Palgrave-Macmillan, 2010.
17. Office for National Statistics. 'Outcomes for Disabled People in the UK: 2020'. *Office for National Statistics*, 18 February 2021. https://www.

ons.gov.uk/peoplepopulationandcommunity/healthandsocialcare/
disability/articles/outcomesfordisabledpeopleintheuk/2020

18. Shulamite A. Green, and Ayelet Ben-Sasson. 'Anxiety Disorders
    and Sensory Over-Responsivity in Children with Autism Spectrum
    Disorders: Is There a Causal Relationship?' *Journal of Autism and
    Developmental Disorders* 40, no. 12 (2010): 1495–1504. https://doi.
    org/10.1007/s10803-010-1007-x

19. Differentnotdeficient. 'Sensory Survival: Living with Hypersensitivity,
    Overwhelm, & Meltdowns'. *Neuroclastic*, 28 April 2019. https://
    neuroclastic.com/sensory-survival-living-with-hypersensitivity-
    overwhelm-meltdowns/

20. Robert Hassan. *Empires of Speed: Time and the Acceleration of Politics
    and Society*. Boston: Brill Academic, 2009, 20–21.

21. Berardi, *Soul at Work*, 108.

22. Ahmad Ghanizadeh. 'Sensory Processing Problems in Children with
    ADHD, A Systematic Review'. *Psychiatry Investigation* 8, no. 2 (2011):
    89–94. https://doi.org/10.4306/pi.2011.8.2.89

23. Raphaelle Beau-Lejdstrom, Ian Douglas, Stephen J. W. Evans, and
    Liam Smeeth. 'Latest Trends in ADHD Drug Prescribing Patterns in
    Children in the UK: Prevalence, Incidence and Persistence'. *BMJ Open*
    6 (2016): e010508. https://bmjopen.bmj.com/content/6/6/e010508

24. Russell A. Barkley, Kevin R. Murphy, and Mariellen Fischer. *ADHD in
    Adults: What the Science Says*. New York and London: The Guildford
    Press, 2008, 279.

25. Stefano Tancredi, Teresa Urbano, Marco Vinceti, and Tommaso
    Filippini. 'Artificial Light at Night and Risk of Mental Disorders: A
    Systematic Review'. *Science of The Total Environment* 833 (2022):
    155–185. https://doi.org/10.1016/j.scitotenv.2022.155185

26. Eliana Neophytou, Laurie A. Manwell, and Roelof Eikelboom.
    'Effects of Excessive Screen Time on Neurodevelopment, Learning,
    Memory, Mental Health, and Neurodegeneration: A Scoping Review'.
    International Journal of Mental Health and Addiction 19, no. 3 (2021):
    724–744. https://doi.org/10.1007/s11469-019-00182-2

27. Manfred E. Beutel, Claus Jünger, Eva M. Klein, Philipp Wild, Karl
    Lackner, Maria Blettner, Harald Binder et al. 'Noise Annoyance Is
    Associated with Depression and Anxiety in the General Population
    – The Contribution of Aircraft Noise'. *PLoS ONE* 11, no. 5 (2016):
    e0155357. https://doi.org/10.1371/journal.pone.0155357

28. Roianne R. Ahn, Lucy Jane Miller, Sharon Milberger, and Daniel N.
    McIntosh. 'Prevalence of Parents' Perceptions of Sensory Processing
    Disorders Among Kindergarten Children'. *American Journal*

of Occupational Therapy 58, no. 3 (2004): 287–293. https://doi. org/10.5014/ajot.58.3.287

29. Harvey Goldstein. 'Francis Galton, Measurement, Psychometrics and Social Progress'. *Assessment in Education: Principles, Policy & Practice* 19, no. 2 (2012): 156. https://doi.org/10.1080/0969594X.2011.614220

30. Kurt Danziger. *Constructing the Subject: Historical Origins of Psychological Research.* Cambridge: Cambridge University Press, 1990, 112–113.

31. For instance, the author of this book once failed a personality test when applying to work as a kitchen assistant for a well-known British pub chain.

32. Anne Parsons. *From Asylum to Prison: Deinstitutionalisation and the Rise of Mass Incarceration after 1945.* Chapel Hill: The University of North Carolina Press, 2018, 3.

33. Ryan Hatch. *Silent Cells: The Secret Drugging of Captive America.* Minneapolis: University of Minnesota Press, 2019, 11.

34. Liat Ben-Moshe. 'Why Prisons are not "The New Asylums."' *Punishment & Society* 19, no. 3 (2017). https://doi.org/10.1177/1462474517704852

35. Mark Fisher. *Capitalist Realism: Is There No Alternative?* Ropley: Zero Books, 2009, 19.

36. Fisher, *Capitalist Realism*, 37.

37. A. Gustavsson, M. Svensson, F. Jacobi, C. Allgulander, J. Alonso, E. Beghi, R. Dodel, M. Ekman, C. Faravelli, L. Fratiglioni, B. Gannon, D. H. Jones, P. Jennum, A. Jordanova, L. Jönsson, K. Karampampa, M. Knapp, G. Kobelt, T. Kurth, and R. Lieb. 'Cost of Disorders of the Brain in Europe 2010'. *European Neuropsychopharmacology: The Journal of the European College of Neuropsychopharmacology*, 21, no. 10 (2011): 720. https://doi.org/10.1016/j.euroneuro.2011.08.008

38. Ari Ne'eman. 'Screening Sperm Donors for Autism? As an Autistic Person, I Know That's the Road to Eugenics'. *The Guardian*, 30 December 2015. www.theguardian.com/commentisfree/2015/dec/30/screening-sperm-donors-autism-autistic-eugenics

39. Anne E. McGuire. 'Buying Time: The S/pace of Advocacy and the Cultural Production of Autism'. *Canadian Journal of Disability Studies* 2, no. 3 (2013): 114. https://doi.org/10.15353/cjds.v2i3.102

40. P. R. Heck, D. J. Simons, and C. F. Chabris. '65% of Americans Believe they are Above Average in Intelligence: Results of two Nationally Representative Surveys'. *PLoS ONE*, 13 no. 7 (2018). Article e0200103. https://doi.org/10.1371/journal.pone.0200103

41. Martha Nussbaum. *Frontiers of Justice: Disability, Nationality, Species Membership.* Cambridge: Belknap Press, 2006, 364–365.

42. Jeremy Appel. 'The Problems with Canada's Medical Assistance in Dying Policy'. *Jacobin*, 8 January 2023. https://jacobin.com/2023/01/canada-medically-assisted-dying-poverty-disability-eugenics-euthanasia

CHAPTER 9

1. Judy Singer. *NeuroDiversity: The Birth of an Idea*, Self-published, Amazon, 2016, 18.
2. Steve Silberman. *NeuroTribes: The Legacy of Autism and the Future of Neurodiversity*. New York: Avery, 2015.
3. Judy Singer. 'Why Can't You be Normal for Once in Your Life?: From a "Problem with No Name" to a New Category of Disability'. In *Disability Discourse*, edited by Mairian Corker and Sally French, 59–67. Buckingham: Open University Press, 1999, 64.
4. Union of Physically Impaired Against Segregation and The Disability Alliance. 'Fundamental Principles of Disability'. London: UPIAS, 1975, 4.
5. Sami Schalk. *Black Disability Politics*. Durham: Duke University Press, 2022, 34.
6. Jim Sinclair. 'Don't Mourn for Us'. *Our Voice* 1, no. 3 (1993). www.autreat.com/dont_mourn.html
7. Harvey Blume. 'Neurodiversity: On the Neurological Underpinnings of Geekdom'. *The Atlantic*, September 1998. www.theatlantic.com/magazine/archive/1998/09/neurodiversity/305909/
8. Judy Singer. 2018. 'Neurodiversity: Definition and Discussion'. *Reflections on Neurodiversity*. https://neurodiversity2.blogspot.com/p/what.html
9. Thomas Kuhn. *The Structure of Scientific Revolutions*. 50th anniversary ed. Chicago: University of Chicago Press, 2012.
10. Nick Walker, and Dora Raymaker. 'Toward a Neuroqueer Future: An Interview with Nick Walker'. *Autism in Adulthood* 3, no. 1 (2021): 6. https://doi.org/10.1089%2Faut.2020.29014.njw

CHAPTER 10

1. Steve Graby. 'Neurodiversity: Bridging the Gap Between the Disabled People's Movement and the Mental Health System Survivors' Movement?' In *Madness, Distress and the Politics of Disablement*. Bristol, UK: Policy Press, 2015. https://doi.org/10.51952/9781447314592.ch016

2. Lydia X. Z. Brown, and Shain M. Neumeier. 'In the Pursuit of Justice: Advocacy by and for Hyper-Marginalized People with Psychosocial Disabilities through the Law and Beyond'. In *Mental Health, Legal Capacity, and Human Rights*, edited by Michael Ashley Stein, Faraaz Mahomed, Vikram Patel, and Charlene Sunkel, 332–348. Cambridge: Cambridge University Press, 2021. https://doi.org/10.1017/9781108979016.025

3. Remi M. Yergeau. *Authoring autism: on rhetoric and neurological queerness*. Durham, NC, Duke University Press, 2017.

4. J. Davies. *Sedated: How Modern Capitalism Created Our Mental Health Crisis*. London: Atlantic Books, 2021.

5. Frantz Fanon. *The Wretched of the Earth*. Translated by Constance Farringdon. Harmondsworth: Penguin, 1967.

6. Karina Zapata. Decolonizing mental health: The importance of an oppression-focused mental health system. *Calgary Journal*. 2020. https://calgaryjournal.ca/2020/02/27/decolonizing-mental-health-the-importance-of-an-oppression-focused-mental-health-system/

7. Beatrice Adler-Bolton, and Artie Vierkant. *Health Communism: A Surplus Manifesto*. Brooklyn: Verso, 2022.

8. M. Cresswell, and H. Spandler. 'Psychopolitics: Peter Sedgwick's Legacy for Mental Health Movements'. *Social Theory and Health* 7, no. 2, (2009): 129–147.

9. Recovery In the Bin, 'About Us'. https://recoveryinthebin.org/

10. Mark Fisher. *Capitalist Realism: Is There No Alternative?* Ropley: Zero Books, 2009.

11. Chapman, 'The Reality of Autism'.

12. Zentall et al., 'Social Behavior in Cooperative Groups'.

13. Robert Chapman. 'Neurodiversity and the Social Ecology of Mental Functions'. *Perspectives on Psychological Science*, 16, no. 6 (2021): 1360–1372. doi:10.1177/1745691620959833

14. Karl Marx. *Grundrisse: Foundations of the Critique of Political Economy*. Translated by Martin Nicolous. Aylesbury: Penguin Books, 1993, 706.

15. Harvey Blume. 'Neurodiversity: On the Neurological Underpinnings of Geekdom'. *The Atlantic*, September 1998. www.theatlantic.com/magazine/archive/1998/09/neurodiversity/305909/

16. Jasbir Puar. *The Right to Maim: Debility, Capacity, Disability*. Durham: Duke University Press, 2017, 79.

CHAPTER 11

1. Raya Dunayevskaya. 'The Union of Soviet Socialist Republics is a Capitalist Society'. *The Marxist-Humanist Theory of State Capitalism:*

Selected Writings. Chicago: News and Letters, 1992. www.marxists. org/archive/dunayevskaya/works/1941/ussr-capitalist.htm

2. Vladimir Lenin. 'Concerning The Conditions Ensuring the Research Work of Academician I. P. Pavlov and His Associates: Decree of the Council of People's Commissars'. In *Lenin's Collected Works.* 1st English ed. Volume 32. Translated by Yuri Sdobnikov. Moscow: Progress Publishers, 1965, 69. www.marxists.org/archive/lenin/works/cw/pdf/lenin-cw-vol-32.pdf

3. Victor Sebestyen. *Lenin: The Man, the Dictator, and the Master of Terror.* New York: Pantheon Books, 2017, 484.

4. Nikolai Krementsov. *With and Without Galton: Vasilii Florinskii and the Fate of Eugenics in Russia.* Cambridge: Open Book Publishers, 2018.

5. Leon Trotsky. 'If America Should Go Communist'. 17 August 1934. www.marxists.org/archive/trotsky/1934/08/ame.htm

6. Paul Raekstad. *Karl Marx's Realist Critique of Capitalism Freedom, Alienation, and Socialism.* Switzerland, Palgrave Macmillan, 2022, 25. https://doi.org/10.1007/978-3-031-06353-4

7. Janine Booth. 'Marxism and Autism', 2017. www.janinebooth.com/content/marxism-and-autism

Bibliography

Adams, Mark B. 'The Politics of Human Heredity in the USSR, 1920–1940'. *Genome* 31, no. 2 (1989): 879–884. https://doi.org/10.1139/g89-155

Adler-Bolton, Beatrice, and Vierkant, Artie. *Health Communism: A Surplus Manifesto*. Brooklyn: Verso, 2022.

Ahmed, Nabil, Marriott, Anna, Dabi, Nafkote, Lowthers, Megan, Lawson, Max, and Mugehera, Leah. *Inequality Kills: The Unparalleled Action Needed to Combat Unprecedented Inequality in the Wake of COVID-19*. Oxford: Oxfam, 2022. https://policy-practice.oxfam.org/resources/inequality-kills-the-unparalleled-action-needed-to-combat-unprecedented-inequal-621341/

Ahn, Roianne R., Miller, Lucy Jane, Milberger, Sharon, and N. McIntosh, Daniel. 'Prevalence of Parents' Perceptions of Sensory Processing Disorders Among Kindergarten Children'. *American Journal of Occupational Therapy* 58, no. 3 (2004): 287–293. https://doi.org/10.5014/ajot.58.3.287

American Psychiatric Association. *Diagnostic and Statistical Manual of Mental Disorders*. Washington DC: APA Press, 1952.

American Psychiatric Association. *DSM-II: Diagnostic and Statistical Manual of Mental Disorders*. Washington DC: APA Press, 1968.

American Psychiatric Association. *DSM-III: Diagnostic and Statistical Manual*. Washington DC: APA Press, 1980.

Andreasen, Nancy. *The Broken Brain: The Biological Revolution in Psychiatry*. New York and London: Harper & Row, 1984.

Appel, Jeremy. 'The Problems with Canada's Medical Assistance in Dying Policy'. *Jacobin*, 8 January 2023. https://jacobin.com/2023/01/canada-medically-assisted-dying-poverty-disability-eugenics-euthanasia

Asasumasu, Kassiane. 2018. 'PSA from the Actual Coiner of "Neurodivergent"'. https://sherlocksflataffect.tumblr.com/post/121295972384/psa-from-the-actual-coiner-of-neurodivergent

Barkley, Russell A., Murphy, Kevin R., and Fischer, Mariellen. *ADHD in Adults: What the Science Says*. New York and London: The Guildford Press, 2008.

Beau-Lejdstrom, Raphaelle, Douglas, Ian, Evans, Stephen J. W., and Smeeth, Liam. 'Latest Trends in ADHD Drug Prescribing Patterns in

Children in the UK: Prevalence, Incidence and Persistence'. *BMJ Open* 6 (2016): e010508. https://bmjopen.bmj.com/content/6/6/e010508

Bell, Daniel. 'The Study of Man: Adjusting Men to Machines'. *Commentary*, January 1947. www.commentary.org/articles/daniel-bell-2/the-study-of-man-adjusting-men-to-machines/

Ben-Moshe, L. Why prisons Are Not "The New Asylums." *Punishment & Society* 19, no. 3 (2017). https://doi.org/10.1177/1462474517704852

Ben-Moshe, Liat. *Decarcerating Disability: Deinstitutionalization and Prison Abolition*. Minneapolis, Minnesota University Press, 2020.

Berardi, Franco. *The Soul at Work: From Alienation to Autonomy*. Los Angeles: Semiotext(e), 2009.

Bernays, Edward. 'The Engineering of Consent'. *Annals of the American Academy of Political and Social Science* 250, no. 1 (1947): 113–120. https://doi.org/10.1177/000271624725000116

Beutel, Manfred E., Jünger, Claus, Klein, Eva M., Wild, Philipp, Lackner, Karl, Blettner, Maria, Binder, Harald et al. 'Noise Annoyance Is Associated with Depression and Anxiety in the General Population – The Contribution of Aircraft Noise'. *PLoS ONE* 11, no. 5 (2016): e0155357. https://doi.org/10.1371/journal.pone.0155357

Bleuler, Eugen. *Textbook of Psychiatry*. Translated by A. A. Brill. New York: Macmillan, 1924.

Blume, Harvey. 'Neurodiversity: On the Neurological Underpinnings of Geekdom'. *The Atlantic*, September 1998. www.theatlantic.com/magazine/archive/1998/09/neurodiversity/305909/

Boorse, Christopher. 'On the Distinction Between Disease and Illness'. *Philosophy and Public Affairs* 5, no. 1 (1975): 49–68.

Booth, Janine. 'Marxism and Autism', 2017. www.janinebooth.com/content/marxism-and-autism

Boutang, Yann Moulier. *Cognitive Capitalism*. Translated by Ed Emery. Cambridge: Polity Press, 2012.

Brockbank, William. *Portrait of a Hospital, 1752–1948 to Commemorate the Bi-Centenary of the Royal Infirmary, Manchester*. London: William Heinemann, 1952.

Brown, Lydia X. Z., and Neumeier, Shain M. 'In the Pursuit of Justice: Advocacy by and for Hyper-Marginalized People with Psychosocial Disabilities through the Law and Beyond'. In *Mental Health, Legal Capacity, and Human Rights*, edited by Michael Ashley Stein, Faraaz Mahomed, Vikram Patel, and Charlene Sunkel, 332–348. Cambridge: Cambridge University Press, 2021. https://doi.org/10.1017/9781108979016.025

Brydall, John. *Non Compos Mentis: Or, The Law Relating to Natural Fools*. London: Atkins, 1700.

Bush, George H. W. 'Presidential Proclamation 6158'. *Library of Congress*, 17 July 1990. www.loc.gov/loc/brain/proclaim.html

Campbell, Chloe. *Race and Empire: Eugenics in Colonial Kenya*. Manchester: Manchester University Press, 2011.

Campbell, Dennis. 'UK Has Experienced "Explosion" in Anxiety Since 2008, Study Finds'. *The Guardian*, 14 September 2020, https://www.theguardian.com/society/2020/sep/14/uk-has-experienced-explosion-in-anxiety-since-2008-study-finds

Campbell, Dennis. 'One in Four UK Prisoners has Attention Deficit Hyperactivity Disorder, Says Report'. *The Guardian*, 18 June 2022. www.theguardian.com/society/2022/jun/18/uk-prisoners-attention-deficit-disorder-adhd-prison

Cave, Stephen, and Dihal, Kanta. 'Ancient Dreams of Intelligent Machines: 3,000 Years of Robots'. *Nature: Books and Arts*, 25 July 2018. www.nature.com/articles/d41586-018-05773-y#:~:text=The%20French%20philosopher%20Ren%C3%A9%20Descartes,the%20philosopher's%20death%20in%201650

Chamberlin, Judi. *On Our Own: Patient-Controlled Alternatives to the Mental Health System*. New York: Hawthorn Books, 1978.

Chapman, Robert. 'Did Gender Norms Cause the Autism Epidemic?' *Critical Neurodiversity*, 29 November 2016. https://criticalneurodiversity.com/2016/11/29/did-gender-norms-cause-the-autism-epidemic/

Chapman, Robert. 'The Reality of Autism: On the Metaphysics of Disorder and Diversity'. *Philosophical Psychology*, 33, no. 6 (2020): 799–819. https://doi.org/10.1080/09515089.2020.1751103

Chapman, Robert. 'Neurodiversity and the Social Ecology of Mental Functions'. *Perspectives on Psychological Science*, 16, no. 6 (2021): 1360–1372. doi:10.1177/1745691620959833

Cipriani, Andrea, Toshi, Furukawa, Salanti, Georgia, Chaimani, Anna, Atkinson, Lauren Z., Ogawa, Yusuke, Leucht, Stefan, Ruhe, Henricus G., Turner, Erick H., Higgins, Julian P., Egger, Matthias, Takeshima, Nozomi, Hayasaka, Yu, Imai, Hissei, Kiyomi, Shinohara, Tajika, Aran, Ioannidis, John P. A., and Geddes, John R. 'Comparative Efficacy and Acceptability of 21 Antidepressant Drugs for the Acute Treatment of Adults with Major Depressive Disorder: A Systematic Review and Network Meta-Analysis'. *The Lancet* 391, no. 10128 (2018): 1357–1366. https://doi.org/10.1016/S0140-6736(17)32802-7

Cooper, David G., ed. *The Dialectics of Liberation*. Harmondsworth: Penguin, 1968.

Cooper, David G. *Psychiatry and Anti-Psychiatry*. Abingdon: Routledge, 2001.

Cresswell, M. and Spandler, H. 'Psychopolitics: Peter Sedgwick's Legacy for Mental Health Movements'. *Social Theory and Health* 7, no. 2, (2009): 129–147.

Cryle, Peter M., and Stephens, Elizabeth. *Normality: A Critical Genealogy*. Chicago: University of Chicago Press, 2018.

Danziger, Kurt. *Constructing the Subject: Historical Origins of Psychological Research*. Cambridge: Cambridge University Press, 1990.

Darwin, Charles. *On the Origin of Species by Means of Natural Selection, Or, The Preservation of Favoured Races in the Struggle for Life*. London: John Murray, 1859.

Davis, Lennard J. *Enforcing Normalcy: Disability, Deafness, and the Body*. London: Verso, 1995.

Davies, J. *Sedated: How Modern Capitalism Created Our Mental Health Crisis*. London: Atlantic Books, 2021.

Descartes, René. *Meditations on First Philosophy with Selections from the Objections and Replies*. Translated by Michael Moriarty. Oxford: Oxford University Press, 2008.

Differentnotdeficient. 'Sensory Survival: Living with Hypersensitivity, Overwhelm, & Meltdowns'. *Neuroclastic*, 28 April 2019. https://neuroclastic.com/sensory-survival-living-with-hypersensitivity-overwhelm-meltdowns/

Dunayevskaya, Raya. 'The Union of Soviet Socialist Republics is a Capitalist Society'. *The Marxist-Humanist Theory of State Capitalism: Selected Writings*. Chicago: News and Letters, 1992. www.marxists.org/archive/dunayevskaya/works/1941/ussr-capitalist.htm

Ebert, Theodor. 'Did Descartes Die of Poisoning?' *Early Science and Medicine* 24, 2 (2019): 142–185, https://doi.org/10.1163/15733823-00242P02

Elizabeth I. 'An Act for the Relief of the Poor'. 1601. www.workhouses.org.uk/poorlaws/1601act.shtml

Fanon, Frantz. *The Wretched of the Earth*. Translated by Constance Farringdon. Harmondsworth: Penguin, 1967.

Farrar, Frederic William. 'Review of *Hereditary Genius* by Francis Galton'. *Fraser's Magazine* 2 (1870): 251–265.

Federici, Silvia. *Caliban and the Witch: Women, the Body and Primitive Accumulation*. New York: Autonomedia, 2004.

Ferguson, Iain. *Politics of the Mind: Marxism and Mental Distress*. London: Bookmarks, 2017.

Finkelstein, Vic. 'Disability and the Helper/Helped Relationship'. In *Handicap in a Social World*, edited by Ann Brechin, Penny Liddiard, and John Swain. Sevenoaks: Hodder & Stoughton, 1981. Reprinted

at   https://disability-studies.leeds.ac.uk/wp-content/uploads/sites/40/
   library/finkelstein-Helper-Helped-Relationship.pdf
Fisher, Mark. *Capitalist Realism: Is There No Alternative?* Ropley: Zero
   Books, 2009.
Foot, John. *The Man Who Closed the Asylums: Franco Basaglia and the
   Revolution in Mental Health Care.* London: Verso Books, 2015.
Foucault, Michel. *Madness and Civilization: A History of Insanity in the Age
   of Reason.* New York: Vintage Books, 2006.
Freud, Sigmund. *The Psychopathology of Everyday Life.* Translated by James
   Strachey. Harmondsworth: Penguin Books, 1975.
Friedlander, Henry. *The Origins of Nazi Genocide: From Euthanasia to the
   Final Solution.* Chapel Hill and London: University of North Carolina
   Press, 1995.
Galton, Francis. *Hereditary Genius: An Inquiry into its Laws and
   Consequences.* London: Macmillan, 1869.
Galton, Francis. 'The History of Twins, as a Criterion of the Relative Powers
   of Nature and Nurture'. *Fraser's Magazine* 12 (1875): 556–576.
Galton, Francis. *Natural Inheritance.* 5th ed. New York: Macmillan, 1894.
Galton, Francis. *Memories of My Life.* London: Methuen, 1908.
Galton, Francis. *Inquiries into Human Faculty and Its Development.*
   London: Everyman, 1907. https://galton.org/books/human-faculty/
   SecondEdition/text/web/human-faculty4.htm#_Toc503102656
Ghanizadeh, Ahmad. 'Sensory Processing Problems in Children with
   ADHD, A Systematic Review'. *Psychiatry Investigation* 8, no. 2 (2011):
   89–94. https://doi.org/10.4306/pi.2011.8.2.89
Goldstein, Harvey. 'Francis Galton, Measurement, Psychometrics and
   Social Progress'. *Assessment in Education: Principles, Policy & Practice* 19,
   no. 2 (2012): 147–158. https://doi.org/10.1080/0969594X.2011.614220
Goodey, C. F. *A History of Intelligence and 'Intellectual Disability': The
   Shaping of Psychology in Early Modern Europe.* Farnham: Ashgate, 2011.
Grabowski, David C., Aschbrenner, Kelly A., Feng, Zhanlian, and Mor,
   Vincent. 'Mental Illness in Nursing Homes: Variations Across States'.
   Health Affairs 28, no. 3 (2009): 689–700. https://doi.org/10.1377/
   hlthaff.28.3.689
Graby, Steve. 'Neurodiversity: Bridging the Gap Between the Disabled
   People's Movement and the Mental Health System Survivors' Movement?'
   In *Madness, Distress and the Politics of Disablement.* Bristol, UK: Policy
   Press, 2015. https://doi.org/10.51952/9781447314592.ch016
Green, Shulamite A., and Ben-Sasson, Ayelet. 'Anxiety Disorders and
   Sensory Over-Responsivity in Children with Autism Spectrum
   Disorders: Is There a Causal Relationship?' *Journal of Autism and*

Developmental Disorders 40, no. 12 (2010): 1495–1504. https://doi.
org/10.1007/s10803-010-1007-x

Gustavsson, A., Svensson, M., Jacobi, F., Allgulander, C., Alonso, J., Beghi,
E., Dodel, R., Ekman, M., Faravelli, C., Fratiglioni, L., Gannon, B., Jones,
D. H., Jennum, P., Jordanova, A., Jönsson, L., Karampampa, K., Knapp,
M., Kobelt, G., Kurth, T., and Lieb, R., 'Cost of Disorders of the Brain
in Europe 2010'. *European Neuropsychopharmacology: The Journal of
the European College of Neuropsychopharmacology*, 21, no. 10 (2011):
718–779. https://doi.org/10.1016/j.euroneuro.2011.08.008

Hacking, Ian. *The Taming of Chance*. Cambridge: Cambridge University
Press, 1990.

Haque, Amber. Psychology from Islamic Perspective: Contributions
of Early Muslim Scholars and Challenges to Contemporary Muslim
Psychologists. *Journal of Religion and Health* 43, no. 4 (2004): 357–377.

Harvey, David. *A Brief History of Neoliberalism*. Oxford: Oxford University
Press, 2005.

Hassan, Robert. *Empires of Speed: Time and the Acceleration of Politics and
Society*. Boston: Brill Academic, 2009.

Hatch, Ryan. *Silent Cells: The Secret Drugging of Captive America*.
Minneapolis: University of Minnesota Press, 2019.

Hayek, Friedrich A. *The Road to Serfdom: Text and Documents*. Definitive
ed. Edited by Bruce Caldwell. Chicago: University of Chicago Press,
2007.

Heathorn, Stephen. 'Explaining Russell's Eugenic Discourse in the 1920s'.
Russell: The Journal of Bertrand Russell Studies 25, no. 2 (2005): 107–139.
https://doi.org/10.15173/russell.v25i2.2083

Heck, P. R., Simons, D. J., and Chabris, C. F. 65% of Americans Believe
they are Above Average in Intelligence: Results of two Nationally
Representative Surveys. *PLoS ONE*, 13 no. 7 (2018). Article e0200103.
https://doi.org/10.1371/journal.pone.0200103

Hippocrates. *Hippocratic Writings*. Translated by G. E. R. Lloyd, John
Chadwick, and W. N. Mann. Harmondsworth: Penguin, 1984.

Hochschild, Arlie Russell. *The Managed Heart: Commercialization of
Human Feeling*. Berkeley: University of California Press, 2012.

Horkheimer, Max, and Adorno, Theodor. *Dialectic of Enlightenment:
Philosophical Fragments*. Edited by Gunzelin Schmid Noerr. Translated
by Edmund Jephcott. Stanford: Stanford University Press, 2002.

Horwitz, Allan V. *What's Normal? Reconciling Biology and Culture*. New
York: Oxford University Press, 2016.

Hunt-Kennedy, Stefanie. 'Imagining Africa, Inheriting Monstrosity:
Gender, Blackness, and Capitalism in the Early Atlantic World'. In

Between Fitness and Death, 13–38. Champaign: University of Illinois Press, 2020. https://doi.org/10.5622/illinois/9780252043192.003.0002

Hunt-Kennedy, Stefanie. 'Unfree Labor and Industrial Capital: Fitness, Disability, and Worth'. In *Between Fitness and Death*, 69–94. Champaign: University of Illinois Press, 2020. https://doi.org/10.5622/illinois/9780252043192.003.0004

Hunter, Edward. 'Brain-Washing Tactics Force Chinese into Ranks of the Communist Party'. *Miami News*, 24 September 1950.

Itandala, Buluda. 'Feudalism in East Africa'. *Utafiti: Journal of the Faculty of Arts and Social Sciences* 8, no. 2 (1986): 29–42.

Jarrett, Simon. *Those They Called Idiots: The Idea of the Disabled Mind from 1700 to the Present Day*. London: Reaktion Books, 2020.

Keller, Richard. 'Madness and Colonization: Psychiatry in the British and French Empires, 1800–1962'. *Journal of Social History* 35, no. 2 (2001): 295–326.

Knifton, Lee, and Inglis, Greig. 'Poverty and mental health: policy, practice and research implications'. *BJPsych Bulletin* 44, no. 5 (2020): 193–196. http://doi.org/10.1192/bjb.2020.78

Kõlves, Kairi, Fitzgerald, Cecilie, Nordentoft, Merete, Wood, Stephen James, and Erlangsen, Annette. 'Assessment of Suicidal Behaviors Among Individuals with Autism Spectrum Disorder in Denmark'. *JAMA Network Open* 4, no. 1 (2021): 1–17. http://doi.org/10.1001/jamanetworkopen.2020.33565

Kovel, Joel. *The Enemy of Nature: The End of Capitalism or the End of the World?* New York: Zed Books, 2002.

Krementsov, Nikolai. *With and Without Galton: Vasilii Florinskii and the Fate of Eugenics in Russia*. Cambridge: Open Book Publishers, 2018.

Kraepelin, Emil. 'Ends and Means of Psychiatric Research'. *Journal of Mental Science* 68, no. 281 (1922): 115–143. https://doi.org/10.1192/bjp.68.281.115

Kraepelin, Emil. *Memoirs*. Edited by Hanns Hippius, G. Peters, and Detlev Ploog. Berlin: Springer-Verlag, 1987. https://doi.org/10.1007/978-3-642-71924-0

Kuhn, Thomas. *The Structure of Scientific Revolutions*. 50th anniversary ed. Chicago: University of Chicago Press, 2012.

Lemov, Rebecca. *World as Laboratory: Experiments with Mice, Mazes, and Men*. New York: Hill and Wang, 2005.

Lenin, Vladimir. 'Concerning The Conditions Ensuring the Research Work of Academician I. P. Pavlov and His Associates: Decree of the Council of People's Commissars'. In *Lenin's Collected Works*. 1st English ed. Volume 32. Translated by Yuri Sdobnikov. Moscow: Progress Publishers, 1965, 69. www.marxists.org/archive/lenin/works/cw/pdf/lenin-cw-vol-32.pdf

Liu, Qingqing, He, Hairong, Yang, Jin, Feng, Xiaojie, Zhao, Fanfan, and Lyu, Jun. 'Changes in the Global Burden of Depression from 1990 to 2017: Findings from the Global Burden of Disease Study'. *Journal of Psychiatric Research* 126 (2020): 134–140. https://doi.org/10.1016/j.jpsychires.2019.08.002

Mackenzie, Donald. *Statistics in Britain 1865–1930 The Social Construction of Scientific Knowledge*. Edinburgh, Edinburgh University Press, 1981.

Marcuse, Herbert. *One-Dimensional Man: Studies in the Ideology of Advanced Industrial Society*. Boston: Beacon Press, 1964.

Marcuse, Herbert. *Soviet Marxism: A Critical Analysis*. London and Aylesbury: Routledge & Kegan Paul, 1969.

Marx, Karl. 'Estranged Labour'. *Economic and Philosophical Manuscripts of 1844*. *Marxists Internet Archive*, 1844. www.marxists.org/archive/marx/works/1844/manuscripts/labour.htm

Marx, Karl. *The Karl Marx Library, Volume I*. Edited by Saul K. Padover. New York: McGraw Hill, 1972.

Marx, Karl. *Capital: A Critique of Political Economy, Volume I*. Translated by Ben Fowkes. London: Penguin Books, 1990.

Marx, Karl. *Capital: A Critique of Political Economy, Volume III*. Translated by Ben Fowkes and David Fernbach. London: Penguin, 1990.

Marx, Karl. *Grundrisse: Foundations of the Critique of Political Economy*. Translated by Martin Nicolous. Aylesbury: Penguin Books, 1993.

Maudsley, Henry. *The Physiology and Pathology of the Mind*. New York: Appleton, 1867.

Mazumdar, Pauline M. H. *Eugenics, Human Genetics and Human Failings: The Eugenics Society, Its Sources and its Critics in Britain*. London and New York: Routledge, 1992.

McGuire, Anne E. 'Buying Time: The S/pace of Advocacy and the Cultural Production of Autism'. *Canadian Journal of Disability Studies* 2, no. 3 (2013): 98–125. https://doi.org/10.15353/cjds.v2i3.102

McGuire, Coreen. *Measuring Difference, Numbering Normal: Setting the Standards for Disability in the Interwar Period*. Manchester: Manchester University Press, 2020.

McLeod, Alexus. 'Chinese Philosophy has Long Known that Mental Health is Communal'. *Psyche*, 1 June 2020. https://psyche.co/ideas/chinese-philosophy-has-long-known-that-mental-health-is-communal

McNally, Richard. *What is Mental Illness?* Cambridge: Belknap Press, 2011.

Mills, Charles Wright. *White Collar: The American Middle Classes*. 50th anniversary ed. New York: Oxford University Press, 2002.

Moser, Dan, and Grant, Allan. 'Screams, Slaps and Love: A Surprising, Shocking Treatment Helps Fargone Mental Cripples'. *Life*, 7 May 1965.

Nadesan, Majia Holmer. *Constructing Autism: Unravelling the 'Truth' and Understanding the Social*. London: Routledge, 2005.

Ne'eman, Ari. 'Screening Sperm Donors for Autism? As an Autistic Person, I Know That's the Road to Eugenics'. *The Guardian*, 30 December 2015. www.theguardian.com/commentisfree/2015/dec/30/screening-sperm-donors-autism-autistic-eugenics

Neophytou, Eliana, Manwell, Laurie A., and Eikelboom, Roelof. 'Effects of Excessive Screen Time on Neurodevelopment, Learning, Memory, Mental Health, and Neurodegeneration: A Scoping Review'. *International Journal of Mental Health and Addiction* 19, no. 3 (2021): 724–744. https://doi.org/10.1007/s11469-019-00182-2

Nussbaum, Martha. *Frontiers of Justice: Disability, Nationality, Species Membership*. Cambridge: Belknap Press, 2006.

Office for National Statistics. 'Outcomes for Disabled People in the UK: 2020'. *Office for National Statistics*, 18 February 2021. www.ons.gov.uk/peoplepopulationandcommunity/healthandsocialcare/disability/articles/outcomesfordisabledpeopleintheuk/2020

Oliver, Michael. *The Politics of Disablement*. London: Macmillan Education, 1990.

Parsons, Anne. *From Asylum to Prison: Deinstitutionalisation and the Rise of Mass Incarceration after 1945*. Chapel Hill: The University of North Carolina Press, 2018.

Pavlov, Ivan. *The Work of the Digestive Glands*. London: Griffin, 1902.

Plato. *Phaedrus*. Translated by Alexander Nehamas and Paul Woodruff. Indianapolis: Hackett, 1995.

Porter, Roy. 'Foucault's Great Confinement'. *History of the Human Sciences* 3, no. 1 (1990): 47–54. https://doi.org/10.1177/095269519000300107

Proctor, Robert. *Racial Hygiene: Medicine under the Nazis*. Cambridge, MA, and London: Harvard University Press, 1988.

Puar, Jasbir. *The Right to Maim: Debility, Capacity, Disability*. Durham: Duke University Press, 2017.

Quetelet, Adolphe. *A Treatise on Man and the Development of His Faculties*. Translated by R. Knox. Edited by T. Smibert. Cambridge: Cambridge University Press, 2014. https://doi.org/10.1017/CBO9781139864909

Raekstad, Paul, *Karl Marx's Realist Critique of Capitalism Freedom, Alienation, and Socialism*. Switzerland, Palgrave Macmillan, 2022. https://doi.org/10.1007/978-3-031-06353-4

Raper, Simon. 'The Shock of the Mean'. *Significance* 14, no. 6 (2017): 12–17. https://doi.org/10.1111/j.1740-9713.2017.01087.x

Reich, Wilhelm. *The Mass Psychology of Fascism*. New York: Orgone Institute Press, 1946.

Rekers, George, and Lovaas, Ivar. 'Behavioral Treatment of Deviant Sex-Role Behaviors in a Male Child'. *Journal of Applied Behavior Analysis* 7, no. 2 (1974): 173–190. https://doi.org/10.1901/jaba.1974.7-173

Robinson, Cedric J. *Black Marxism: The Making of the Black Radical Tradition*. London: Penguin Modern Classics, 2021.

Robison, John Elder. 'Kanner, Asperger, and Frankl: A Third Man at the Genesis of the Autism Diagnosis'. *Autism* 21, no. 7 (2017): 862–871.

Rogers, Adam. 'Star Neuroscientist Tom Insel Leaves the Google-Spawned Verily for [...] a Startup?' *Wired*, 11 May 2017. www.wired.com/2017/05/star-neuroscientist-tom-insel-leaves-google-spawned-verily-startup/?mbid=social_twitter_onsiteshare

Rosenthal, Caitlin. 'Slavery's Scientific Management'. In *Slavery's Capitalism*, edited by Seth Rockman and Sven Beckert, 62–86. Philadelphia: University of Pennsylvania Press, 2016.

Russell, Ginny, Stapley, Sal, Newlove-Delgado, Tamsin, Salmon, Andrew, White, Rhianna, Warren, Fiona, Pearson, Anita, and Ford, Tamsin. 'Time Trends in Autism Diagnosis over 20 Years: A UK Population-based Cohort Study'. *Journal of Child Psychology and Psychiatry* 63, no. 6 (2021): 674–682. https://doi.org/10.1111/jcpp.13505

Timimi, Sami, McCabe, Brian, and Gardner, Neil. *The Myth of Autism: Medicalising Mens' and Boys' Social and Emotional Competence*. Basingstoke: Palgrave-Macmillan, 2010.

Schalk, Sami. *Black Disability Politics*. Durham: Duke University Press, 2022.

Scull, Andrew. 'Madness and Segregative Control: The Rise of the Insane Asylum'. *Social Problems* 24, no. 3 (1977): 337–351. https://doi.org/10.2307/800085

Scull, Andrew. *Decarceration: Community Treatment and the Deviant – A Radical View*. Hoboken: Prentice-Hall, 1977.

Scull, Andrew. *Madness in Civilization: A Cultural History of Insanity, from the Bible to Freud, from the Madhouse to Modern Medicine*. Princeton: Princeton University Press, 2016.

Scull, Andrew. *Desperate Remedies: Psychiatry's Turbulent Quest to Cure Mental Illness*. Cambridge, MA: Harvard University Press, 2022.

Sebestyen, Victor. *Lenin: The Man, the Dictator, and the Master of Terror*. New York: Pantheon Books, 2017.

Sedgwick, Peter. *Psychopolitics: Laing, Foucault, Goffman, Szasz, and the Future of Mass Psychiatry*. London: Unkant, 2015.

Silberman, Steve. *NeuroTribes: The Legacy of Autism and the Future of Neurodiversity*. New York: Avery, 2015.

Sinclair, Jim. 'Don't Mourn for Us'. *Our Voice* 1, no. 3 (1993). www.autreat.com/dont_mourn.html

Singer, Judy. 'Why Can't You be Normal for Once in Your Life?: From a "Problem with No Name" to a New Category of Disability'. In *Disability Discourse*, edited by Mairian Corker and Sally French, 59–67. Buckingham: Open University Press, 1999.

Singer, Judy. *NeuroDiversity: The Birth of an Idea*, Self-published, Amazon, 2016.

Singer, Judy. 2018. 'Neurodiversity: Definition and Discussion'. *Reflections on Neurodiversity*. https://neurodiversity2.blogspot.com/p/what.html

Skinner, Burrhus Frederic. *The Behavior of Organisms*. New York: Appleton-Century-Crofts, 1938.

Skinner, Burrhus Frederic. *Beyond Freedom and Dignity*. Bungay: Pelican, 1976.

Sloarch, Roddy. *A Very Capitalist Condition: A History and Politics of Disability*. London: Bookmarks, 2016.

Sneed, Debby. 'The Architecture of Access: Ramps at Ancient Greek Healing Sanctuaries'. *Antiquity* 94, no. 376 (August 2020): 1015–1029. https://doi.org/10.15184/aqy.2020.123

Spitzer, Robert L. 'The Diagnostic Status of Homosexuality in DSM-III: A Reformulation of the Issues'. *American Journal of Psychiatry* 138, no. 2 (1981): 210–215. https://doi.org/10.1176/ajp.138.2.210

Staub, Michael E. *Madness is Civilisation: When the Diagnosis Was Social, 1948–1980*. Chicago and London: University of Chicago Press, 2011.

Stern, Alexandra Minna. 'Making Better Babies: Public Health and Race Betterment in Indiana, 1920–1935'. *American Journal of Public Health* 92, no. 5 (2002): 742–752. https://doi.org/10.2105%2Fajph.92.5.742

Stewart, John. '"The Dangerous Age of Childhood": Child Guidance in Britain c.1918–1955'. *History & Policy*, 1 October 2012. www.historyandpolicy.org/policy-papers/papers/the-dangerous-age-of-childhood-child-guidance-in-britain-c.1918-1955

Stopes, Marie Carmichael. *Radiant Motherhood: A Book for Those Who Are Creating the Future*. London: G. P. Putnam's Sons, 1921.

Straton, James. *Contribution to the Mathematic of Phrenology: Chiefly Intended for Students*. Aberdeen: William Russell, 1845.

Sysling, Fenneke. 'Phrenology and the Average Person, 1840–1940'. *History of the Human Sciences* 34, no. 2 (2021): 27–45. https://doi.org/10.1177/0952695120984070

Szasz, Thomas. 'The Myth of Mental Illness'. *American Psychologist* 15, no. 2 (1960): 113–118. https://doi.org/10.1037/h0046535

Szasz, Thomas. Letters to Friedrich August von Hayek, 1964–1983. *The Thomas S. Szasz, M.D. Cybercenter for Liberty and Responsibility*. www.szasz.com/hayek.html

Szasz, Thomas. 'An Autobiographical Sketch'. In *Szasz Under Fire: The Psychiatric Abolitionist Faces His Critics*. Edited by Jeffrey A. Schaler, 1–28. Chicago: Open Court, 2004.

Szasz, Thomas. *Psychiatry: The Science of Lies*. New York: Syracuse University Press, 2008.

Tancredi, Stefano, Urbano, Teresa, Vinceti, Marco, and Filippini, Tommaso. 'Artificial Light at Night and Risk of Mental Disorders: A Systematic Review'. *Science of The Total Environment* 833 (2022): 155–185. https://doi.org/10.1016/j.scitotenv.2022.155185

Taylor, Stephen, Annand, Fizz, Burkinshaw, Peter, Greaves, Felix, Kelleher, Michael, Knight, Jonathan, Perkins, Clare, Tran, Anh, White, Martin, and Marsden, John 'Dependence and Withdrawal Associated with Some Prescribed Medicines: An Evidence Review'. *Public Health England*, London. 2019. https://assets.publishing.service.gov.uk/government/uploads/system/uploads/attachment_data/file/940255/PHE_PMR_report_Dec2020.pdf

Terlizzi, Emily, and Norris, Tina. 'Mental Health Treatment Among Adults: United States, 2020'. *NCHS Data Brief* 419 (2021). https://dx.doi.org/10.15620/cdc:110593external icon

Thatcher, Margaret. 'Interview for *Catholic Herald*, 5 December 1978'. *Margaret Thatcher Foundation*. www.margaretthatcher.org/document/103793

Thatcher, Margaret. 'Nicholas Ridley Memorial Lecture'. Central London, 22 November 1996. *Margaret Thatcher Foundation*. www.margaretthatcher.org/document/108368

Torrey, E. Fuller, and Yolken Robert, H. 'Psychiatric Genocide: Nazi Attempts to Eradicate Schizophrenia'. *Schizophrenia Bulletin* 36, no. 1 (2010): 26–32. https://doi.org/10.1093/schbul/sbp097

Trotsky, Leon. 'If America Should Go Communist'. 17 August 1934. www.marxists.org/archive/trotsky/1934/08/ame.htm

Turner, David M., and Blackie, Daniel. *Disability in the Industrial Revolution: Physical Impairment in British Coalmining, 1780–1880*. Manchester: Manchester University Press, 2018.

Union of Physically Impaired Against Segregation and The Disability Alliance. 'Fundamental Principles of Disability'. London: UPIAS, 1975.

Walker, Nick. 'Throw Away the Master's Tools: Liberating Ourselves from the Pathology Paradigm'. In *Loud Hands: Autistic People, Speaking*. Edited by J. Bascom, 225–237. Washington: Autistic Self Advocacy Network, 2012.

Walker, Nick, and Raymaker, Dora. 'Toward a Neuroqueer Future: An Interview with Nick Walker'. *Autism in Adulthood* 3, no. 1 (2021): 5–10. https://doi.org/10.1089%2Faut.2020.29014.njw

Wallace, Alfred R. Review of *Hereditary Genius, an Inquiry into its Laws and Consequences* by Francis Galton. *Nature* 1 (1870): 501–503. https://doi.org/10.1038/001501a0

Watson, John. *Behaviorism*. New York: People's Institute, 1924.

Watts, Sheldon. *Disease and Medicine in World History*. London: Routledge, 2003.

Watters, Ethan. *Crazy Like Us: The Globalization of the Western Mind*. St Ives: Robison, 2011.

Webb, Sidney. *The Difficulties of Individualism*. London: The Fabian Society, 1896.

Whitaker, Robert. *Anatomy of an Epidemic: Magic Bullets, Psychiatric Drugs, and the Astonishing Rise of Mental Illness in America*. New York: Crown, 2010.

Yergeau, Remi, M. *Authoring autism: on rhetoric and neurological queerness*. Durham, NC, Duke University Press, 2017.

Zapata, Karina. Decolonizing mental health: The importance of an oppression-focused mental health system. *Calgary Journal*. 2020. https://calgaryjournal.ca/2020/02/27/decolonizing-mental-health-the-importance-of-an-oppression-focused-mental-health-system/

Zentall, S. S., Craig, B. A., and Kuester, D. A. 'Social Behaviour in Cooperative Groups: Students at Risk for ADHD and their Peers'. *Journal of Educational Research* 104 (2011): 28–41. https://doi.org/10.1080/0892 4562.2018.1465869

Acknowledgements

Given various contingent historical occurrences and bourgeois ideology, books tend to be attributed to single authors. In reality they are always the product of collective effort. This book has gone through many transformations, and along the way has been shaped, guided, and improved by a great many people.

Various parts of the book have, at different points, been significantly strengthened following feedback from Hane Maung, Coreen McGuire, David Batho, Koshka Duff, Shelley Tremain, Havi Carel, Jaakko Nevasto, Shona Murphy, Chris Bailey, Tuomas Pernu, Tom Whyman, John Ray, Alice McAndrew, Anton Jäger, Judy Singer, Isaac Kneebone Hopkins, and Nick Walker. At relatively late stages, extensive and invaluable feedback on the whole draft was provided by Joshua Habgood-Coote, Beatrice Adler-Bolton, David Shulman, and Hel Spandler.

I have also gained much from informal interactions with everyone already noted, but also countless others. These include Micha Frazer-Caroll, Abs Stannard Ashleigh, Monique Botha-Kite, Justin Garson, Nipper Mad Dog, Nev Jones, Virginia Bovell, Dan Degerman, David Mordecai, Alastair Morgan, Vincenzo Passantre Spaccapietra, RoseAnnieFlo, Guilaine Kinouani, Béatrice Han-Pile, Damian Milton, Sonia Soans, Steven Kapp, Jay Watts, Fergus Murray, Sonny Hallet, Abdo Abuhassan, and far too many others to mention. They will each surely disagree with me on much, but their insights permeate throughout.

Over the past year, I wrote much of the book while stuck in bed with Long Covid. During this time, while his editorial suggestions have been rejected, my cat Marcel has been a constant and steadfast companion. Special thanks also go to my editor, David Shulman, who has provided unwavering support and guidance from the moment we first spoke.

Finally, I would never have been able to have written this book without Alice, Jenny, Adrian, Harriet, Daniel, and Dan. I cannot thank them enough for everything they have done and continue to do.

Index

Thanks to our Patreon subscriber:

Ciaran Kane

Who has shown generosity and comradeship in support of our publishing.

Check out the other perks you get by subscribing to our Patreon – visit patreon.com/plutopress.

Subscriptions start from £3 a month.